D1230078

BEESON
PASTORAL SERIES

LEADING IN TIMES OF CHANGE

DALE GALLOWAY
AND BEESON INSTITUTE COLLEAGUES

Beacon Hill Press of Kansas City
Kansas City, Missouri

Copyright 2001 by Beacon Hill Press of Kansas City

ISBN: 083-411-917X

Printed in the United States of America

Cover Design: Paul Franitza

Unless otherwise indicated, all Scripture quotations are taken from the *Holy Bible, New International Version*® (NIV®). Copyright © 1973, 1978, 1984 by International Bible Society. Used by permission of Zondervan Publishing House. All rights reserved.

Permission to quote from the following additional copyrighted versions is acknowledged with appreciation:

The *New American Standard Bible*® (NASB®), © copyright The Lockman Foundation 1960, 1962, 1963, 1968, 1971, 1972, 1973, 1975, 1977, 1995.

The *New King James Version* (NKJV). Copyright © 1979, 1980, 1982 Thomas Nelson, Inc.

The *New Revised Standard Version* (NRSV) of the Bible, copyright 1989 by the Division of Christian Education of the National Council of the Churches of Christ in the USA. All rights reserved.

The *Living Bible* (TLB), © 1971. Used by permission of Tyndale House Publishers, Inc., Wheaton, IL 60189. All rights reserved.

King James Version (KJV)

Library of Congress Cataloging-in-Publication Data
Galloway, Dale E.
  Leading in times of change / Dale Galloway and Beeson Institute colleagues.
    p. cm.—(Beeson pastoral series)
  ISBN 0-8341-1917-X
  1. Church management. 2. Christian leadership. 3. Change—Religious aspects—Christianity.
I. Title. II. Series.
  BV652.1 .G34 2001
  253—dc21
                                                                    2001043347

10 9 8 7 6 5 4 3 2 1

Contents

Acknowledgments

Effective change agents always have allies. The seven contributors to this book, myself included, could not have led churches through transition without the partnership of many influencers, unfortunately too numerous to name. Only God knows the important role each of them played! All of us—Dale Galloway, John Maxwell, Elmer Towns, Mike Breaux, William Hinson, Gene Appel, and Jim Garlow—deeply thank God for these friends and acknowledge that our journey of faith would not have been possible without them.

I also want to acknowledge the role my office team has played in helping me host the Beeson Institute for Advanced Church Leadership, and then compile and edit this series of messages from it. All of these ministries occur through the encouragement and blessing of my good friend Maxie Dunnam, who is president of our parent organization, Asbury Theology Seminary.

Warren Bird serves as my in-house editor and liaison with the publisher. The Beeson Center team that assists us is Penny Ruot, Stephanie Hall, Ellen Frisius, and Heather McPherson. My longtime friend Neil Wiseman, working for the publisher, prepares the first draft of the manuscript. Then the fine team at Beacon Hill, under the leadership of Bonnie Perry, gives the book its final form and puts it in your hands.

I also thank my partner-in-life, Margi Galloway, who has added much smoothness and grace to the transitions we've led various ministries through over the years.

Introduction

I've always had a passion for church planting. In recent years God has also given me a strong passion for helping pastors to transition older, dying churches. Both approaches are essential to the strategy for reaching as many people as possible with the gospel today.

Such researchers as Win Arn have documented that 80 to 85 percent of North American churches are plateaued or dying. That means four of five churches will be gone—or irrelevant—if they don't transition. Some will sell their buildings to a library or different religion, while others will continue meeting, lifeless, but not knowing that they lack spiritual vitality.

The opening chapter of this book quotes Sam Shoemaker, the Episcopal priest influential in the founding of Alcoholics Anonymous. He asked, "Can your kind of church change your kind of world?" If it can't, it must change in order to become effective in today's world. It's lunacy to continue to do the same kind of thing and expect different results.

Leaders must do more than merely realize the need for transition. It is imperative that we know how to introduce planned change. A Boeing 747 airplane can bank 33 degrees and the passengers hardly notice it. At 45 degrees the passengers become uncomfortable, but at 90 degrees the pilot will crash the plane. I want readers to get a handle on how to turn their "plane" at 33 degrees.

If you load a gravel truck too fast, it will sink or be damaged. If you gradually fill it up, it will absorb and handle the new cargo. We have to learn as change agents to introduce change in a gradual way.

No one transitions without making some mistakes, and hopefully you can learn from all the mistakes described in these chapters.

The contributors to this book are church leaders who have been effective in producing change in a wide range of different settings. You'll learn all kinds of "unchangeable" change principles that will help you.

• In the opening *Dale Galloway* chapter, I summarize the most important ideas that work from the four churches I've pastored over three decades.

• *John Maxwell* offers outstanding advice about how to walk people through transition and change.

• *Elmer Towns* has been up close to more change agents over five decades than anyone else I know.

• *Mike Breaux* tells how he led a church through major transitions when his predecessor's shadow was everywhere he went.

• *Bill Hinson*, *Gene Appel*, and *Jim Garlow* write from the context of frontline churches. Each has a distinct kind of story. Each is amazing in what they faced—and in what God did. Each will fill you with hope that God can use you as a successful change agent.

Several places in the book reference the Beeson Institute for Advanced Church Leadership. This is a group of several hundred pastors who meet together at different teaching churches across the country. Each of these chapters was presented at one of those gatherings, where I serve as dean. If you need more help in transitioning, I invite you to join one of the Beeson Institute series. For a complimentary brochure or video contact toll free 888-5BEESON or 859-858-2307, E-mail <beeson_institute@asbury seminary.edu>, or visit our web site at <www.asburyseminary.edu>, and then click "site index" for the Beeson Institute.

I look forward to hearing what God does in the congregation you serve as you become a more effective change agent.

▪ *1* ▪

PROFILE OF A SUCCESSFUL CHANGE AGENT

Dale E. Galloway

We major on trying to retain what we have always done just so we will not have to take a chance.
—George Barna

Glade Run Presbyterian Church presents itself as "the NEW church that's been around for 200 years." According to Chris Marshall, senior pastor, the congregation has made a genuine change "from surviving to thriving." This church in Valencia, Pennsylvania, evidences a new sense of vitality in every area—from children's ministry to corporate worship.

Kingswood United Methodist Church, Amarillo, Texas, has likewise benefited from its pastor's learning to be a change agent. Pastor Terry Tamplen reports that Kingswood's attendance has increased 30 percent over the last two years. "We've moved from the old paradigm, where my staff and I did the ministry, to a better model of lay leaders' stepping up, getting excited about their church and faith, taking ownership of the vision, reaching out, and using their spiritual gifts," he says.

CHANGE PROCESS BEGINS WITH "ME"

In every case study I can remember, the pastoral leaders have discovered the same starting point for where the change process must begin. To be an effective change agent, the first person who needs to change is "me."

My book *Leading with Vision* (Beacon Hill, 1999) explains how at every point of growing a church, I had to adjust. Before I could lead the church to the next step, I had to change the way I spent time and approached ministry.

One of my in-residence Beeson pastors, Dan Reinhardt, personalized the question for the church he serves: "How do I have to change as a leader to take my church from 1,000 to 2,000 in worship attendance?"

Some pastors, like the cork in a bottle, won't let anything out. Their approach amounts to "containing" ministry through their personal control of everything possible.

Some pastors resist change because of a pessimism toward those who buck it. These pastors view their congregations as being stupid, closed minded, lazy, stubborn, and hostile. However, in such cases the pastor's attitude is the real momentum killer. A leader must be a person of faith who sees beyond, who has a positive, possibility-believing spirit. A mind-set of negativity can drag anyone down.

Some leaders need a sense of desperation or pain before being willing to change. The largest church in the world, Yoido Full Gospel in Seoul, developed its approach to lay ministry because of Pastor David Yonggi Cho's emotional and physical breakdown. Out of his brokenness and pain he began to emphasize lay pastors and small groups.

In my 32 years of pastoring, two of the churches I served were long-established congregations. Frankly, I didn't have the acquired wisdom or skills to successfully lead them through transition.

Every adversity gives us striking opportunities for personal enlargement and growth.

In the first church, everything I tried hit the wall. I felt as if I were a car driver spinning his tires and going nowhere. This sense of zero progress resulted in a frustrating learning experience. However, I learned about small-group ministry, a concept that served me well in years to come.

The next church had averaged 200 people for 30 years, and it grew to about 300 during my tenure. Then I experienced a personal family crisis.

Every adversity gives us striking opportunities for personal enlargement and growth. Through these difficult times I learned to focus on love as my No.1 aim in both life and ministry.

THREE CRUCIAL CHANGE PERSPECTIVES

Chris Marshall, Terry Tamplen, Dan Reinhardt, and thousands of other pastors have taken great strides toward becoming more effective change agents. So can you.

Some say that leadership ability springs from something in the genes: "Either you've got it, or you don't." Researcher Peter Drucker disagrees. He notes that strong leaders more often emerge as they learn the right things and become good at them.

Drucker also stresses three important perspectives the change agent should take:

1. Eternal truth never changes. Any number of scriptures underscore this idea. "Jesus Christ is the same yesterday and today and forever" (Heb. 13:8). "Heaven and earth will pass away, but my words will never pass away" (Luke 21:33). "I am not ashamed of the gospel, because it is the power of God for the salvation of everyone who believes" (Rom. 1:16).

2. Culture is rapidly changing. Ken Blanchard, coauthor of the *One-Minute Manager,* says, "The thinking that got you to where you are today will not take you where you need to be tomorrow." It is important to notice what is no longer working and to find a new breakthrough.

Culture keeps changing, and we must know and respond to those changes, or the church will turn into an old relic that lacks relevance or influence.

3. Tools and methods change. Many sections of the Bible teach that God is a God of freshness and change. "And no one pours new wine into old wineskins. If he does, the new wine will burst the skins, the wine will run out and the wineskins will be ruined. No, new wine must be poured into new wineskins" (Luke 5:37-38). New "wineskins" are essential, not optional, if you intend to communicate the gospel to this generation. Learn and stand firm on biblically based principles and core values, but keep learning new methods to effectively communicate these to your culture.

Some things never change. Some things always do. And some things *need* to change.

UNDERTAKER, CARETAKER, RISK TAKER

I believe that basically three approaches to pastoring exist. The *undertaker* tends to serve a church that's *traditional* in the sense of same, same, same all the time. The undertaker spends a lot of time burying folks.

The *caretaker* leads a *transitional* church. Caretakers help change the focus from programs to people, from rituals to relationships.

Finally, the *risk taker* is on the cutting edge, reaching people for Christ. The risk taker leads a *transformational* church.

What happens in our own spirit determines more than anything else whether we will win or lose in our efforts to introduce planned change.

If you want to become a transformational, risk-taking leader, here are some of the skills you will need to develop:

1. **Possess the gift of leadership.** Everything rises and falls on leadership. Too many people think they are leaders, but in reality they only maintain the status quo. Li Hung-chang said, "There are three kinds of people: those who are moveable, those who are unmovable, and those who move them."

2. **Have an authentic walk with God.** What happens in our own spirit determines more than anything else whether we will win or lose in our efforts to introduce planned change. According to Richard Kriegbaum in *Leadership Prayers,* the person wanting to become a leader will "pray to maintain the right relationship with God. From that relationship between the human spirit and the spirit of God comes the divine perspective, insight, direction, and courage the leader must have to serve well. Ulti-

mately, prayer determines the leader's effectiveness in what matters most—the eternal matters of the human spirit, including the leader's own spirit."

3. Become a visionary leader. As Ken Blanchard says, we have to maintain the "realist" perspective of having one foot in the present and the "unreasonableness" of having the other foot in the future. George Bernard Shaw said reasonable people "adapt to their environment," while unreasonable people "try to adapt their environment to themselves." He concluded that "all progress" is the result of unreasonable people.

4. Develop an appropriate sense of inadequacy. If we don't reach beyond ourselves, we become self-sufficient. Rom. 12:3 (TLB) says, "As God's messenger I give each of you God's warning: Be honest in your estimate of yourselves, measuring your value by how much faith God has given you." Our only guarantee of success comes from our relationship with God. "I can do all things through Christ who strengthens me" (Phil. 4:13, NKJV).

5. Have supportive families that really like you. Risk takers don't neglect their marriage and kids. Mike Breaux, my pastor at Southland Christian Church, Lexington, Kentucky, one Sunday announced that he was going to spend more time with his family, even coaching one of his children's sports teams. The church at the time was experiencing some major changes, making it especially important for the pastor's family life to remain healthy.

6. Do not be satisfied with the status quo. Cutting-edge leaders think outside the box. They show a holy discontent with church as usual. Sometimes successful change agents tend to feel lonely. Sometimes people feel a bit uncomfortable around them. These leaders also tend to have a sense of urgency about them.

7. Demonstrate a great passion for the lost. These pastors really love lost people. Things happen because they have a "fire in the belly" as the prophets of old had. Or as the expression Sylvester Stallone uses in *Rocky* goes, nothing will take the place of that "eye of the tiger."

8. Show commitment to core values. People who hang around effective change agents quickly learn that these leaders have clearly set core values. They know how to keep the main thing as the main thing. They show an ability to see the big picture. They keep the church centered on the Great Commission and the Great Commandment by asking the right questions.

9. Learn not to take negative reactions personally. Effective leaders are both tough skinned and tender. It doesn't come easy for me to separate my identity and work from my role as pastor and leader. Ministry is in my soul. If people are negative about what God wants the church to do, I have trouble with their negativity. I came to understand that often people do not react to me personally but to the role of pastor. As my dad continually advised, "You've got to become tough skinned if you're going to make it in ministry."

10. Love all people, especially those resisting change. It's easy to love those who share our ideals. Tony Campolo tells the story of a mother and daughter flying home. The little girl had snacked on soda and chocolate-chip cookies, and then air disturbance set in. She threw up all over her dress, and it really stank. As she got off the plane, everyone but her mother moved away from her. "Dad," waiting to meet them as they got off the plane, wore a clean, white suit. The daughter saw him. He ran toward her, saying, "Honey, I love you. I missed you." She got the mess all over his suit, but he didn't seem to care. Campolo's conclusion: A leader's biggest test is whether we can love the people puking all over us!

CHANGE: A DO-OR-DIE ISSUE

Lyle Schaller's book *Discontinuity and Hope* emphasizes that many churches will die if they don't change. "The trends of the 1990s suggest that the congregations near the top of the endangered ecclesiastical species list are the churches averaging 85 to 200 in worship." Quite a sizable percentage of today's congregations!

He says the greatest need is for people who learn change-agent skills. He also acknowledges that this presents a tough challenge. "Nearly all will agree that being an effective parish pastor is far more difficult today than it was 40 years ago," he says.

It may take more skill to transition a church than it does to plant a church. You need church-planting skill plus the ability to understand the church's culture. "The wisest approach to planned change," says Schaller, is to design a strategy "that includes considerable continuity with the past."

That reality calls for an increasing number of pastors to develop the profile of a change agent.

Urgent call: Needed now. Pastors and leaders who will become change agents to save these dying churches, while simultaneously reaching out to save the unchurched. Is that you?

TAKING THE MYSTERY OUT OF CHANGE

"Anyone seriously interested in planned social change would be well advised to recognize two facts of life. First, despite the claims of many, relatively little is known about how to achieve predictable change. Second, much of what is known will not work."

Lyle Schaller published those words in 1972 in *The Change Agent*. They are still true.

How, then, do you learn how to lead your church forward through the delicacies of the change process? Business expert Joel Barker says a good leader often develops instincts for and an intuition of what works and what doesn't work.

The same holds true in ministry. I learned what would reach people and what wouldn't. You, too, can develop those senses. First Chron. 12:32 highlights the men of Issachar whom God gifted to understand the "times and [know] what Israel should do." Through God's empowerment you, too, can become a student of change.

The following "change realities" should take some of the mystery out of the change process. Then four questions will guide you in how to lead your church from where it stands now to where it needs to go next.

Ten Change Realities

1. **An unchanging church does not exist.** All living organisms, whether plants, animals, or people, are subject to the phenomenon of life cycles. They are born, grow, age, and die. The same proves true for the congregation you serve. It's always changing for better or worse.

2. **Without change there is no change.** It is lunacy to do the same thing over and over and expect different results. Sam Shoemaker, the Episcopal priest influential in the founding of Alcoholics Anonymous, asked, "Can your kind of church change

your kind of world?" If it can't, it must change in order to become effective in today's world.

3. Change cannot occur without discomfort and pain. Human nature generally avoids most kinds of hurt, but wise leaders know how to lead a congregation ahead into the unknown. Maxie Dunnam, a longtime pastor and the current president of Asbury Theological Seminary, writes this in *Let Me Say That Again:* "Most of us prefer the hell of a predictable situation rather than risk the joy of an unpredictable one."

4. Perception becomes reality. I remember hearing a layperson describe the fund-raising drive at his church. He explained how the pastor set the pace by announcing that he would sell his much-loved boat and donate all the proceeds to the building fund. Yet two months later, according to this lay leader, the pastor was sporting a new, more luxurious boat. "He claimed he was making a sacrifice, but I guess he wasn't," the lay leader observed.

The church didn't know that the pastor had been given the boat by a relative.

The implication? It may not be fair or right, but if something becomes a church's perception, it's as good as reality.

5. What people don't understand, they'll be against. Many times opposition simply means that people don't comprehend the idea behind or the benefits of a proposed change. A lawyer named Therman Arnold once said, "Unhappy is a people that have run out of words to describe what is going on."

6. The reason the change feels uncomfortable is that it usually means giving up something of the past. For many people, change equals loss.

*Transition is the psychological
process people go through to come
to terms with new situations.*

7. Change is a process. As motivational speaker John Maxwell says, people change in three environments: "When they hurt enough that they have to change; when they learn enough that they want to change; or when they receive enough that they are able to change." According to my friend, veteran pastor Stan Toler, "The quality-improvement process is progressive. A church doesn't go from 'terrible' to 'wonderful' in a single week."

8. It isn't the change that does you in; it's the transition. According to William Bridges in *Managing Transition,* the transition period, not the change, will do you in. Change is external, transition internal. Change does not equal transition. Change is situational: the new boss, new team role, and new policy. Transition is the psychological process people go through to come to terms with new situations.

For example, when Margi and I relocated from Portland, Oregon, to my present post at Asbury Theological Seminary, the 2,500-mile drive took us less than a week. But the transition took a long time—months and probably years. For the first month, we'd go to church and cry because we missed being at New Hope Community Church. Then after we left the church services, we'd spend the rest of the day moping around.

After being here a couple of months Margi said to me, "You know, you have a hole to plant your tree in, but I don't." She was right; I came to an awaiting job and she didn't. Sometimes transitions require only a short time, but for me this time I've needed several years. And I don't know if I'm done yet!

9. Not everyone will adapt to change at the same rate. Everett Rogers' book *Diffusion of Innovations* contains a widely reprinted chart that shows how people respond to a new idea. A few jump on early, but many wait until after the majority have adopted it. Each type of personality needs a different level of understanding and help. People may resist change initially, but eventually most can adapt to it. (In the next chapter John Maxwell comments further on this idea—see pages 27-28.)

10. A method of ministry that works successfully in one church or community may not work in another. Often a community's culture and church's culture differ. So even if something worked in your town, it may not work for your church.

I know the pastor of a congregation in rural Idaho. The church's worship attendance plummeted from 800 to 300 in six months. Why? He attended a conference at a high-visibility church and came home wanting to change everything. He had a great heart, but he didn't understand the importance of his community culture and his church culture.

Four Guiding Questions

What **do I need to change?** Armed with these 10 perspectives on change, a church needs to be repeatedly told and sold on the ways in which change needs to happen to get to where God is leading it next. As a leader you can take the mystery out of change and hit a grand-slam home run in making your church a winner in today's world. To do so, you must lead your people in touching all four of these essential bases: *what, why, how,* and *when.*

First, you can sow the seeds of change by emphasizing *what* God calls a church to become and achieve. In casting that vision, which of the following shifts does your congregation most need to make?

- From maintenance to mission
- From death to life
- From the past to the future
- From being ingrown to being outgoing
- From surviving to thriving
- From complacency to urgency
- From no growth to abundant growth

As you question these important areas and establish biblically based core values, you will build a positive basis for change.

U nless they see a need for change, the people will not budge.

While prayerfully pinpointing the right *what* question, continually evaluate your church's situation. What do you know about its history and life cycle? Can you identify its land mines? What do your people value? What are they committed to? What's their level of commitment?

Why **should we change?** Throughout the change process, you must give people a continual answer to the *why* question. To lead people through the emotional experience of change, explain what happens if the church doesn't change and what happens if it does. A good formula for this: If we don't do this, then a such and such serious consequence will happen. For example, "If we don't launch some new worship teams, our musically gifted newcomers will drop out because they won't find a place of service."

Unless they see a need for change, the people will not budge. They will say, "Why do we need to change? We like things the way they are."

That's why leaders are proactive. They want to guard against the pull of gravity. They know that coasting can only take them downhill. If churches keep coasting, they die.

Challenge your people to "greater things than these" (John 14:12). Help them grasp an idea of the benefits that will happen because of the change. For example, suppose you've just taught from Luke 15 that lost people matter to God. You could conclude, "By experimenting with such and such [the change under consideration], we can reach lost people whom God loves and you care about. This could be your neighbor, son or daughter, or grandchildren."

How do we frame the change? I summarize the *how* concept with four Ps: purpose it, picture it, plan it, and play it out, giving everyone a part.

One way to map out the *how:* Arrange all the needed changes according to priority. Think through the process you need to put in place to successfully implement the change or changes.

Remember that the older the church, the longer the process will take. A continuity with the timeless values of the past while communicating and implementing constructive components for the future provides balance for the process.

In another way to bring effective change, you develop two tracks for the church to run on simultaneously—the older or existing model and the newer one.

A classic example involves the worship service. If you're trying to introduce innovation, often the best strategist leaves the traditional services alone. As Charles Arn advises in *How to Start a New Service,* try a new-style service if it has a greater possibility of reaching your target population than your current worship style. If that new service strikes a responsive chord, you may then need to add another new-style service or a Saturday night service as well. Over time the newer track may become so popular that the older track fades away without a great sense of congregational disappointment or loss.

When do we make the change? As in real estate sales, timing is everything. I remember introducing the idea of a Saturday night service at New Hope Community Church. Naively, I didn't rally everyone behind it. I hadn't prepared the people for it, solicited the choir, planned for the children's activities, or challenged 200 people to commit to it. I simply assumed that people would come because of my preaching ability.

I was wrong. It flopped. About six months into our Saturday night service, I realized I hadn't built ownership in it. So we discontinued it.

From that experience and others, I've learned to wait through these top 10 timing circumstances before launching a change:

1. When you have taken the time to hear from the Lord.

2. When you have developed and earned a trust relationship with your people.

3. When you have cultivated among the most influential leaders a strong sense that the church needs change.

4. When you have underscored a corporate dissatisfaction with things as they are.

5. When as a leader you have accumulated "pocket change" from doing several previous things well.

6. When you have caught and built momentum. (When you've got the "Big Mo," you can make changes you can't make at other times.)

7. When you have framed a sense of urgency.

8. When you can genuinely say that the situation demands action right now.

9. When you have built a high level of commitment to the needed change.

10. When you have helped the people understand that the proposed changes are in their best interest.

Remember that if you wait until everything seems perfect,

you'll miss the striking opportunity. Nothing for the better happens until you take risks. You have everything to gain from the right kind of change and nothing to lose.

We serve a God who specializes in doing the impossible. Hotel entrepreneur Conrad Hilton said, "If you want to launch big ships, go to where the water is deep." Dream big, and then lead your congregation to be all God calls it to be.

▪2▪

THE ART OF LEADING PEOPLE THROUGH CHANGE

John Maxwell

*Those who have changed the universe have
never done it by changing officials,
but always by inspiring the people.*
—Napoléon Bonaparte

Assembly Minutes
June 19, 1908

Mr. Grueber introduced the following to be discussed:

Nine reasons not to introduce the typewriter into our church.

1. The paper must be put into the machine and aligned properly, tabs must be set. This is not easy. When writing by hand, one simply begins, exactly where you want with no restrictions.

2. With a typewriter, you have to constantly remember to capitalize and put in punctuation. It is easy to forget, and to go back and change things is hard. When writing by hand, such things are automatic.

3. With the typewriter, you have to have been trained to find the proper keys. This takes time. We already know how to write.

4. With the typewriter, you are limited to the size and spacing of the type. When writing by hand, you can use any size letters or style you want.

23

5. With the typewriter, centering and setting margins is not easy; when writing, it is no problem.

6. A typewriter breaks down and costs to be fixed. Writing does not.

7. Correcting a mistake after something has been typed is a problem; when writing by hand, it is not.

8. The church has gotten along for over 1900 years without a typewriter; why do we need this now?

9. Instead of learning a machine with all the above drawbacks, time should be spent on penmanship.

RESISTANCE TO CHANGE IS ALMOST UNIVERSAL

The typewriter story makes us chuckle nervously. If we wonder why, perhaps it reminds us of our resistance to change. Or maybe we suspect similar situations take place in contemporary churches.

Either way, an important question follows—how does a Christian leader prevent churches from repeating something like the typewriter story over and over?

Three realities that force change in churches are crystal clear: (1) change takes place through and for people, (2) the church must reinvent itself in every generation, and (3) change is as much about leaders as organizations. Christian business leader Max Depree's insight provides a kind of cornerstone for working with these three realities: "We cannot become what we want to be by remaining what we are" (John Woods, ed., *Quotable Executive*).

Why people resist change. At a time in contemporary culture when nearly everything seems caught up in a whirling tornado of change, many congregants have experienced difficult, painful, and frustrating change efforts in their churches in the past. As a result, they feel pessimistic and sometimes angry about all the pain and confusion aborted change efforts have caused them and their families. Out of those experiences, they have developed an almost unexplainable distrust toward anyone who proposes change, including the minister. They think they have good reason to worry that more changes may cause too much carnage.

Another reason is that many church members are unsure of

their leader's competence. They fear their pastor may be inexperienced and/or the lay decision-making group is unsure when it comes to change in the church. Many of these grand people have been dragged through reorganizations, strategy redirection, and false promises of renewal. And they are change weary.

No wonder they are unsure and skeptical. These people need assurance, not ridicule. They need encouragement, not judgment. They need acceptance, not rejection.

Change crowds all of us. Let's move even closer to the change issue. Change beguiles and threatens nearly everyone, especially church members and pastors. No one is immune. Sometimes fear of change makes cowards out of otherwise courageous people. Sometimes a new situation makes wimps out of otherwise brave folks. Frequently, change causes wonderfully well-balanced human beings to act in strange or even volatile ways.

Change fools and misleads some of us all the time and all of us some of the time.

Not even the most progressive person present at the voters' assembly during the discussion against typewriters could have imagined the future. No one could have foreseen the important part the typewriter and its second cousins—electric typewriters and now computers—would play in contemporary society. Likewise, none of us can imagine how changes we resist today will shape society and the church tomorrow.

Even leaders resist change. Change even seduces many ministers into believing they love change. What they actually love is change they initiate. Though they may not be fully aware of it, many pastors are as resistant to change as anyone else. In every field of leadership, including the ministry, unchanged leaders usually end up leading uninteresting status quo, stagnate, or inert organizations.

For robust church health the true leader must be open to new ideas and ready to consider new concepts, which may require change from anyone. Leaders must be willing to change, to change often, and sometimes to change drastically. They must keep reminding themselves that progress starts with change and that change is often required first of the leader before it affects the followers.

That's the pressing problem. Previous generations experienced changes at a much slower pace, so today's leaders who grew up in that era have no legacy to show them how to respond to relentless and fast-moving changes such as we have today. Nevertheless, church people watch to see how their minister responds to change and transitions before they are willing to change.

Leaders often misunderstand reasons for reluctance. Leaders, when deeply committed to great Kingdom causes, sometimes allow themselves to develop a negative mind-set that views the struggle others are having with change as a defect, problem, or flaw—something to be diagnosed, fixed, or attacked. Such a perspective gets the leader nowhere. Therefore, I have three rules about the natural reluctance to change that steer me away from such a negative mind-set.

1. Expect resistance. Human beings inevitably exaggerate the joys of the past, pain of the present, and risks of the future. If that statement is accurate, as I believe it is, then the past gets more positive emotional weight than either the present or the future. It is easy to forget that anything that pushes a person out of his or her comfort zone causes a sense of dread and uncertainty. People who are doing well under existing conditions naturally resist change. Others resist because they do not see a need to change or are unwilling to invest energy in the proposed change because they are not sure it will materialize. Such reactions are perfectly natural.

> *K̲eep the focus on the issues and
> on the advantage of the change
> rather than on relational issues.*

2. Don't take resistance personally. I have made this mistake by wondering, "Why can't they see it. And why don't they just trust me because I am the leader here?" Well, it is just not that simple. People push against change because of their natural reluctance, and it is easy for the leader to think they are resisting him or her rather than reacting to the change.

Keep the focus on the issues and on the advantage of the change rather than on relational issues. Above all else, keep yourself from judging another's motives—only God can do that accurately.

3. *Understand that reluctance sometimes comes in code.* The person who appears to be criticizing the financial cost may really be saying, "I'm scared to death." The one who objects to giving an assignment to a spiritual newcomer may actually be saying, "I don't want to be left out." Resistance to change plays tricks on people because it generally keeps them from thinking and self-evaluation; it sometimes makes habitual reactions to life look silly.

PEOPLE RESPOND TO CHANGE IN MANY WAYS

Everett M. Rogers, journalism professor at the University of New Mexico, wrote a must-read, landmark book titled *Diffusion of Innovations* (New York: Free Press). He helps his readers see the variety of ways people respond to change and shows how to work through the impact their reactions have on an organization and on the leader. He uses five categories.

• **Innovators or dreamers.** These are the idea people who see the possibilities in the change and run with them. They are the venturesome folks who are bright and quick and learn from many fields. They do not need a book or a model. They follow their intuition and the leader's creativity into new ways of doing things. They are usually about 2.5 percent of the population. Ideally, they are key lay leaders and/or members of the staff.

• **Early adopters.** These people take an innovator's idea and build a system to implement the idea and make it flourish. They "get" the new idea from the innovators and make it work. They are approximately 13.5 percent of the population.

• **Early majority.** This group is more deliberate and can be expected to look to opinion-shaping members of the group to gauge the possible effectiveness of the idea. They want to "get it" but also want early adopters to show them where the proposed change is being done effectively. They want books written before you start. Rogers suggests that they are about 34 percent of the population.

• **Later majority.** These are the people who want to see where everyone else is already doing the proposed change. They want to be told exactly how it can be done—point by point. It is not important to them that they "get it." They want to follow and adopt the practices that everyone else has put in place. Obviously, cutting-edge newness is not among their interests. They are about 34 percent of the population.

• **Laggards.** They are determined not to adopt anything new. These are the status quo folks who live in the glories of the past. Often they try and sometimes succeed in creating division within the church to eliminate the proposed change. They are about 16 percent of the population.

> *K eep reminding yourself that you lead the top and middle groups by influencing top leaders and not by debating the bottom resisters.*

Another breakdown from a different source suggests a similar result: Fifteen percent seek out and embrace change like the innovators and early adopters. Fifteen percent resist change like the laggards. That leaves 70 percent who are simply reluctant, like the early majority and later majority. But because there is a great difference between *resistant* and *reluctant,* they can be convinced and involved in change.

What, then, are the implications of these group classifications to change agents? The top 15 percent will go with you on any reasonable change, and the bottom 15 percent won't budge. Keep reminding yourself that the middle group is the key to making change work and that you lead the top and middle groups by influencing top leaders and not by debating the bottom resisters.

If you go back to the typewriter incident, in a church of 300 you have 45 persons pumped and excited about the typewriter, 45 persons dead set against the typewriter, and 210 persons ready to be influenced either way. That means 255 is likely as many as you can expect to support change.

Change the church attendance to 200. You have 30 excited,

30 dead set against it, and 140 willing to be influenced. That means 170 for change is about as good as you will ever get.

Change the church to 100. You have 15 excited, 15 against, and 70 waiting to be influenced. That means 85 for change would be a real victory.

FOUR LEVELS OF CHANGE

Some unknown change-agent leader with years of experience showed a wise understanding of the issues when he said, "Every new idea goes through three phases: it will not work, it will cost too much, and I thought it was a good idea all along." Note that his levels of change acceptance are fluid and dynamic. Clearly, care must be taken not to lock individuals into a category. They can reconsider and change positions and often do.

As a society, and also in the church, we have spent millions and endure considerable pain trying to implement needed changes. We have used TQM (Total Quality Management), self-directed teams, and reengineered organizations. Yet studies show that maybe as much as two-thirds of our change initiatives fail to achieve their intended results.

We must ask why. I believe the answer is simple. We have assumed that change will occur if we can explain where we are trying to go and differentiate that goal from where we are now or where we have been. Wrong. Simply pointing the way from *A* to *B* may have worked in the past. It does not work now because so many changes are behavioral in nature. Accepting change is not made on the basis of logic and good sense alone—acceptance is more often based on people's feelings, experiences, and points of view.

> *Change always goes better and quicker when you have lay leaders supporting proposed changes out of a sense of conviction.*

In our time it is important, therefore, to realize that change-resistant individuals do not usually change in one easy step. Changes are made through a process that moves from facts to feelings to behavioral changes to influencing others.

Here are four levels of change that every leader should pass through.

• **New information is accepted.** This phase of change deals with perspective, which is shaped by receiving the largest amount of information from the greatest number of people. It is the logical outcome of sorting through facts and information before making a change.

• **New attitude is adopted.** This phase relates to feelings people have about proposals and projects. Attitude adjustment is important because it always leads to behavioral changes. Keep in mind that when people are forced to change, a leader should not be surprised if their resistance reappears in the middle of a project.

• **New behavior is practiced.** This phase deals with choices, actions, and the formation of new habits. No real change takes place until it shows in someone's conduct. A conceptual textbook kind of theory concerning change can be discussed for years, but change is not genuine until it shows in conduct.

• **New convictions influence others.** This is the highest phase and deals with investment and ownership. Someone has truly changed when he or she is heard repeating the same rationale given by the leader for making the change. Change always goes better and quicker when lay leaders are supporting proposed changes out of a sense of conviction that this new thing is right and it can be done.

How Change Affects People

To be an effective change agent, it helps to know what happens internally to people as they react and respond to change.

1. **People feel awkward and self-conscious doing something new.** Eric Hoffer, in his book *The Ordeal of Change,* says, "People will cling to an unsatisfactory way of life rather than change in order to get something better for fear of getting something worse." To help make people more comfortable with change, keep saying in every possible way that progress in the church and adventure in life always mean change for someone.

Try to intentionally create a climate in the church where change is seen as a sign of health and vigor. Management specialist Robert H. Waterman in *The Renewal Factor* offers helpful insight: "Healthy organizations, like healthy people, simultaneously experience stability and motion, continuity and change. Too much stability leads to stagnation; too much change results in chaos. Both are decimating, and neither one by itself leads to renewal."

2. People focus on what they have to give up. People want to know how the change will affect them—how will they fit, what will they miss, what visibility will they lose, how much will it cost them, and will they still be needed. Typical examples are comments people make about starting two services, "I will miss seeing part of my church family"; a new small group, "I will lose contact with half the group"; or a rotation system for church board membership, "I have served on that board for 22 years, and I can't imagine not attending those meetings." Notice how these examples show persons who are focused on themselves rather than on the Lord or the people the church should be reaching.

In response, why not teach people the adventure of the trapeze life—it requires letting go in order to move to the next level. In the trapeze life you can laugh at, resist, or embrace the act of moving from one bar to the next, but moving is necessary.

G ive people time to process change.

3. People personalize change and sometimes feel alone in the process. If you see these persons as selfish and immature and say "Get a grip on yourself; we are all in this thing together," they will feel slighted and may even pout awhile. If, however, you understand their response as a human hurt and give love, attention, and understanding, they will process the change more quickly and move ahead.

Most people can identify with French writer Anatole France who said, "All changes, even the most longed for, have their melancholy: for what we leave behind is part of ourselves; we must die to one life before we can enter into another."

4. People are at a different level of readiness for change. Give people time to process change. Everyone processes at a different speed depending on a hundred different issues in his or her inner person. Timing in ministry is significantly more important than most pastors realize. Time the change for the best possible advantage. You do not have to wait for the last person who expressed some reluctance. Neither should you wait for even one laggard, because he or she is not going to support change however long you wait. But for all the others, give them time to adjust to the new ideas and new practices. At first, the issue of readiness sounds complicated for leaders. But almost all people have firsthand experience with this within the families where they grew up. Anyone who has ever been around a child knows that readiness to talk and walk cannot be hurried much. But most people finally do both—and most people will finally accept change too.

SUCCESSFULLY NAVIGATING THE TRANSITIONS

Often the change is not what does the leader or organization in; rather, it is the transition between what was and what is to be that creates problems. It is the time of leaving the old before the new has come.

1. Acknowledge the losses. Many people have never thought about what others may be giving up to allow the change to be implemented. Identify who is losing what, and help each with his or her grief work.

Admit that all losses hurt—some more than others.

Could it be that the losses and endings are the biggest problems most people face rather than a dread of the future and its changes?

Like all grief, the person who suffers loss cannot be argued out of it. Nor should you try. That only stops conversation, damages communication, and drives the hurt underground.

The leader does his or her best work by simply insisting over and over that God is in control and that He will walk with the grieving person through the valley. The leader must also realize that often he or she is seen as the person who created the problem in the first place—thus the healing ministries must sometimes be handed off for someone else to accomplish.

Tend to the people's hearts, and they will follow you through any change. A little hand-holding goes a long way. And an assurance that all will be well takes little effort. The key is to be sensitive and recognize the personal losses. This may be as simple as listening with your heart.

2. Compensate for the losses. That is, give them something more valuable than money. Give them yourself in expressions of genuine concern. Provide those who suffer loss an opportunity to help shape the future so they own the proposed plans. Recognize them for their past contributions. Show how the new programming will be better than the old for them.

In personnel changes, provide a new person who will take the church to higher levels than it ever had been with the previous person. Remember in staff relations, a change is never complete until the new person is in place. A new staff member should be likeable and have the potential for being more effective than the previous leader.

Give people opportunities for personal growth. Many church leaders have had experiences with a few persons who did not want to grow, so they concluded that no one wants to be developed. Many people, perhaps most, want to grow and develop all their lives. Even when they do not know how and do not comprehend the opportunities around them, they still have a desire to grow. Show them how they can grow through the proposed changes, and they may become your friends for life.

Practice good, old-fashioned honesty. Speak about your love for the people. Emphasize the values of human connections, understanding, and care. Tell them the church is the main dispenser of God's grace and enablement.

Communicate unto the other guy that which you would want him to communicate unto you if your positions were reversed."
　　　　　　　　　　　　　—Aaron Goldman

3. Provide people with the maximum amount of information. Share as much data with as many people as possible. Communicate through as many forums as possible—large meetings, small meetings, newsletters, memos, sermons, prayer requests, and informal interactions with people. Become a human well of information.

In every organization, including the church, the confidential issues are incredibly few and far between. Often people think about confidentiality as merely a way to feel as if they know more about something or someone than someone else does. One church leader with a national following said, "Only five percent of what goes on in the church is really confidential, and the five percent is pretty boring."

Though he likely was not thinking about the church, Aaron Goldman, CEO of the Macke Company, offers good advice for Christian leaders: "Communicate unto the other guy that which you would want him to communicate unto you if your positions were reversed" (John Woods, ed. *The Quotable Executive*). Share your vision and plans with as many people as possible.

Some leaders mistakenly think they strengthen and maintain their leadership over an organization by keeping secrets and withholding information. So they tell those who lead only as much as they think those individuals need to do their work.

This policy almost always backfires because those who do not know cannot be held responsible for conduct outside their areas of knowledge—areas that have been made narrow by the secret-keeping leader. Neither can they be helpful in a crisis. Or if they have been shortchanged in their "need to know," they simply say, "I do not know anything about that issue." Then by their tone of voice, they imply that the leader is defective in communication skills. As a result, the big boss finds he or she is leading alone and doesn't even understand why. Pastors do that, too—it's a mistake.

Like the commercial airline pilot who does not share information with the first and second officer in the cockpit, though surrounded by trained personnel with experience, such a leader feels all alone when a crisis hits. No Christian leader can lead alone. It is better to tell the whole story and restudy your position when you meet persistent resistance from fair-minded people.

But the talk has to be understood. Technobabble, specialized theological vocabulary, and "God told me" talk just doesn't help people accept and implement change. Harvard leadership specialist John P. Kotter's fine sentence from *Leading Change* may be applied to the communication of the Christian leader: "Communication seems to work best when it is so direct and so simple that it has a sort of elegance."

4. Clearly define what is over. Explain what remains, what is coming, and what is new. Celebrate the endings. Treat the past with respect. Honor those who have made the present possible through their faithfulness in the past. Call the people to remember that some of the most effective happenings of the past in any congregation came about as a result of change. Honoring the past costs little and accomplishes much. Those who believe in the past with all their hearts will admire your great wisdom. And those who are glad the past is past will believe you are fair minded to speak well of the yesterdays.

How to Win Favor with the People During the Process of Change

Credibility and trust are the most attractive traits to followers who really want to follow their leader. Their belief that you are a decent, good, trustworthy, spiritually mature, honest human being is better than any skill or experience you can bring to your efforts as a change agent. Consistency, full information, and fairness add to the trust level people look for in dependable leaders.

Good ideas can stand the test of discussion.

1. Establish a win record. Make every effort to get smaller leadership wins on your record before you go for big changes. Remember, leadership is earned and not conferred. You may be well trained, ordained, and assigned or elected to a significant position in a church, but you are not a leader until some group believes in you enough to follow you.

People are very slow to follow a leader who speaks of success and future growth if there is no past track record of effectiveness. The following words from Josh Hunt underscore the importance of actual achievement or talk about achievement:

Imagine the leaders of the early church trying to per-

suade the church to follow them into becoming a large mul-
ti-congregational, multi-national church that included
Samaritans and Gentiles. Suppose that after five years of
ministry in Jerusalem, the church had grown from 120 to
165. Some had come in and some had gone. The disciples
were reading over the sayings of Jesus and were reminded of
the Great Commission. They discuss this and tell the
church that they need to develop a missions program to the
Gentiles. What are their chances of pulling off this change?
Right—slim to none!

Contrast this with what actually happened. Several
thousand saved. Success fueled their ability to effect change.

2. **Choose your changes**. Be willing to die for a few
changes and be flexible on everything else. Don't change small
things that do not matter even though you have a different pref-
erence. Give in on little things. The congregation's memory of
your flexibility will serve you well when it comes time to put
your authority on the line for a great change that really matters.

3. **Give generous time for discussion**. Good ideas can stand
the test of discussion. In your church board planning, make room
for information, study, and action items. That gives everyone an
opportunity to offer an opinion and a time to experience the give-
and-take of those who want the best for the church.

4. **Be open and honest in your communication**. Sam Walton, the founder of Wal-Mart, said, "Communicate everything
you possibly can to your partners. The more they understand,
the more they will care. Once they care, there's no stopping
them" (John Woods, ed., *The Quotable Executive*). Walton has a
subtle point that applies to the church as well as to secular business enterprises. The church often thinks about communication
as sharing information, but when its people reach to the caring
level, they are well on their way to becoming like the New Testament church.

5. **Don't fight opposition**. Spend at least 80 percent of your
time shaping the thinking of the majority. Encourage them. Motivate them. Cherish them. Try loving people regardless of their
position on an issue. They will bloom, and you will be blessed.
Eventually, the people will take care of dissenters.

Even though you will eventually have to move on without the footdraggers, let everyone know you want everybody to make the trip together with you. If you run people off by saying something such as "We lost 100 people, but God gave us 200 to replace them," others will think you are running people off. They will believe that you do not have a true pastor's heart, because you so easily wash your hands of spiritual responsibility for people—people whom God loved so much He sent His Son to die for them.

6. **Love and pray for the people daily.** Never allow yourself to get far away from 1 Pet. 5:2-4: "Be shepherds of God's flock that is under your care, serving as overseers—not because you must, but because you are willing, as God wants you to be; not greedy for money, but eager to serve; not lording it over those entrusted to you, but being examples to the flock. And when the Chief Shepherd appears, you will receive the crown of glory that will never fade away."

Though you may not feel like a spiritual giant, that is what people believe you to be. Christlikeness is what they need from you more than anything else.

■3■

HOW TO LEAD YOUR CHURCH THROUGH CHANGE

Dale E. Galloway

*Any child can cry and fret, but it requires
a full-grown man to create and construct.*
—Booker T. Washington

I was invited to a Columbus, Ohio, congregation I had started as a 23-year-old when I was fresh out of seminary. I had begun it by meeting people door-to-door. I had never read a church-planting book, and I didn't really know anything about how to do it. I had just wanted to reach people.

The occasion to which I was now invited was the congregation's move into its new 3,000-seat sanctuary. We gathered that morning in the old worship center—a big, multipurpose room. Packed like sardines, we stood wall-to-wall. Pastor Bobby Huffaker led us in a 10-minute time of thanksgiving to God for all the wonderful things that had happened in that facility. Then we marched over to the new sanctuary and filled it.

I was given a baton and asked to share for 5 minutes about how we started the church. Then I passed the baton to the pastor who had followed me, and it went down the line in that manner.

We had an extended time of worship with conspicuous involvement of youth and children. This part of the service made people feel at home in their new facility.

Toward the conclusion, Pastor Huffaker spoke to me in front of the church. "You built a passion for the lost into the very

DNA of the church," he said. "It has been a dominant character-istic throughout the years and will continue on into the future."

FIFTEEN PRINCIPLES FOR LEADING PRODUCTIVE CHANGE

Behind these kind words, Bobby Huffaker has proven him-self an effective change agent. This new facility service at Grove City Church of the Nazarene and the events that led to it em-body many essential principles for leading a church through the transitions of change.

Let me underscore lessons it has taken me and others a life-time to learn. I hope this list will help minimize your bruises and accelerate the process as you lead your church toward re-newal and increased health.

1. **Repeatedly cast vision.** People volunteer when they catch the vision, and they drop out when they lose it. Vision paints the picture of what God has done and will do. Vision shines like the headlights that point into the future, while pas-sion provides the gas that fuels the engine. As the Book of Acts shows, leadership in the power of the Spirit catalyzes all effective change in the church.

2. **Influence the influencers.** Every church has a power structure. You can try to join it or otherwise change it. A church with a worship attendance of 100 probably has five or six key in-fluencers. In a church with 6,000 in worship, individuals can in-fluence sections of the congregation but not the whole.

3. **Create a "change" leadership team.** John Ed Mathison, pastor of Frazer Memorial United Methodist Church, Montgom-ery, Alabama, calls his change team the "Joel Committee." As Mathison describes in his book *Tried and True,* the Old Testament prophet Joel encouraged the old to dream dreams and the young to see visions (see Joel 2:28). This handpicked group includes the senior pastor and key influencers. It meets at designated times. When this strong, guiding coalition takes its recommen-dations back to other committees, they get accepted.

This is a tremendous idea in an established church. The more you have the key influencers and leaders participating in a leadership team, the easier it is to implement change.

4. **Work with your staff until they become of one mind and heart together.** When John Maxwell went to Skyline Church

in San Diego, he shared his vision and strategy for change. Then he gathered all the staff and asked them, "What would it take on your part to move the church from 1,000 to 2,000 people?"

Questions like that help people buy into the change. By contrast, an inner-city pastor in Cleveland had not been able to develop a goal with his staff. As a result, they undercut everything he did. If you do not get the staff on board with the vision and change, they will eventually sabotage whatever good can happen.

5. **Prepare people for change.** As Lyle Schaller points out in his book *The Interventionist,* the best preparation means asking the right questions. The wise leader creates a dissatisfaction with the status quo, conveying the idea that if the church doesn't change, it can't reach people for Christ. Every cutting-edge church I've studied displays a love and togetherness as a team that allows people to experiment with change.

You always win when you treat the past with respect and build on it.

6. **Affirm the past.** When Mike Breaux came to Southland Christian Church in Lexington, Kentucky, he preached on core values for the first seven weeks. With each sermon he showed how the church of the past carried out a specific value. Then he used that value as a context to teach and cast vision for the future.

You always win when you treat the past with respect and build on it. Doing so blesses the present and prepares for the future. The process of unraveling the way great achievements happened in the past will convince you and your lay leaders that all progress requires a significant change by the congregation.

Without the past, there would be no future. Without a viable future, however, the past would be lost forever.

7. **See it big and keep it simple.** As you communicate the change and vision, give the people a plan they can participate in. Use numerous stories and illustrations. Use multiple formats: meetings, media, written materials, different voices. Use repetition. Use testimonials. Practice what you preach; model it. Keep

the communication going continually. Don't say, "We're going to do away with Sunday night services in order to have small groups." Instead, say, "We are just trying to get more intentional about ministry in our culture." As you repeatedly communicate the vision with clarity and purpose, your people will see the benefits of the proposed change.

8. Overcome complacency with urgency. Complacency and comfort remain the biggest enemies to change. Without a sense of urgency people won't give that extra effort essential to the change process. Turn up the heat with such verses as John 9:4 (KJV): "I must work the works of him that sent me, while it is day." Here is one effective word track to use: "If we don't act now, then *this* will happen." For example:

● "If we don't build this facility for children now, these kids won't be in church tomorrow. What do you think we ought to do?"

● "Think about the women in this congregation. What message do we send by asking them to walk through the mud each week, often with small children in tow, because they have to park out in the field? Is this what we really want?"

● "Every Sunday morning we see would-be guests driving around and then leaving because they have nowhere to park. Can we afford for people who need Jesus not to find a parking spot? What do you think we should do?"

Clarify the urgency behind the need by addressing the why. For example, some 3.5 billion nonbelievers live within reach of existing local churches. What a great reason for not continuing business as usual.

9. Be responsive in leading the people through the adjustment zone of transition. This in-between time can feel like a combat zone, because change often wounds people. It produces pain. I can't tell you how often I've hurt because I knew a change had hurt someone. "No matter how I do it, and no matter how necessary it is, every change hurts someone," says Richard Kriegbaum in *Leadership Prayers*.

Marilyn Ferguson, noted futurist and author, writes in *American Futurist*: "It's not so much that we are afraid of change, or so in love with the old ways, but it's a place in between that we fear. . . . It's like Linus with his blanket in the dryer. There is nothing to hold on to."

When our son Scott was five years old, he had a blanket that he clung to continually. One day we were driving down the freeway and it accidentally flew out the window. There was no way to retrieve it. We immediately bought him a new blanket, but somehow it wasn't like the old one. I thought he'd never go to sleep that night.

If you're having similar experiences in the church you serve, you're not alone. You're experiencing the pains of transitions.

10. Love people through the change. Wise leaders allow for dialogue, inviting people to express their feelings. Be patient. Sometimes people simply need time to catch up with the change.

On one of the Beeson Pastor trips I led to Korea, one of the wives felt terrible. Since we were on a bus, I stood up and began to explain the process of jet lag. Having received permission to feel strained and stretched, she seemed to immediately feel better.

Sometimes people leave a church in order to feel better. It always hurts when people leave because they can't support a change. As they leave, it's important to affirm that you love them, care about them, and will always welcome them back.

Loving others means allowing them to be themselves and to make decisions you may not agree with. Make up your mind that whether your people accept the change or resist it, you will value them, treat them with respect, and show them love.

Choose your battles wisely.

11. Love yourself through the change. Remember—God loves you and has called you to lead the church through the change. Try to separate your personal identity from your role as a change agent. Admit your own failures.

Recognize that you won't please everyone—even God can't do that. Some will leave your church but not the kingdom of God. Others will come and find a new eternity that they wouldn't have otherwise experienced, unless someone had shown the courage to change the way the church reaches out to the contemporary culture.

Choose your battles wisely. Some things aren't worth the battle. Never surrender your leadership to negative, reactionary people. Especially avoid putting those people in up-front roles.

12. Get key lay leaders to shoulder the load and share the vision. When God's people know your heart, they will rise to the challenge. I remember numerous times during my four pastorates when I felt huge pressures. Our people seemed pretty well tapped out, both emotionally and financially, which tempted me to bear the burden alone. However, when I bared my soul and voiced the burden of my heart, people rallied in amazing ways. Often the people of a church are far more willing than their leader realizes to shoulder the load with him or her.

13. Model enthusiasm in your leadership. James Collins, author of *Built to Last,* challenges leaders to articulate BHAGs (pronounced: BEE-hags) for the organizations they serve. This acronym stands for Big, Hairy, Audacious Goals. He shows what can happen through a leader's enthusiasm toward a seemingly impossible challenge. As leaders we want to model Paul's powerful command to "serve the Lord enthusiastically" (Rom. 12:11, TLB). Nothing will happen unless you as a leader get excited about it.

14. Celebrate the victories. Throughout the Old Testament, God instructs His people to celebrate and commemorate times of victory. Even after relatively short accomplishments, such as Nehemiah's 52-day task to rebuild the wall surrounding Jerusalem, they celebrated. It remains important to affirm, "God's doing a great thing." As you point to what God does, also brag on how well the people are doing.

When you don't have such progress and momentum, then you have to live in Heb. 11, talking about what God will do in the future. Take the approach of seeing something before it is. As you start to get results, you can shift, saying "Look at what God is doing," and you celebrate that. Share these "Yea, God" stories often.

15. Stick with the change until it becomes unchangeable reality. Be patient. Remember that progress often comes through three steps forward and two back. The net result: You're still one step ahead! Remember that most people can't make an entire trip in a day.

A transition period, during which the changes become part

of your organizational culture, always follows change. The settling-out period usually runs one to three years and occasionally requires up to five years. This season of adjustments takes time, but it's essential for the changes to remain durable.

Change-agent costs. Is change easy? Almost never. The greater the change, the harder it is to implement. Anything worthwhile has obstacles, and the more worthwhile, the more obstacles you will encounter. However, when God grants the breakthrough, you'll decide that the price paid was worth everything.

TURN YOUR FAILURES INTO STEPPING-STONES

When you think of "failure" in ministry, what kind of person comes to mind? Have you considered the idea that people whom you think successful have often failed the most?

> *People who achieve breakthroughs in ministry don't allow setbacks to discourage them to the point of quitting.*

Babe Ruth, who made his mark as a home-run champion, was also a "strikeout king." Poet Edmund Vance Cooke says, "If you never have failed, it's an easy guess / You never have won any high success."

You don't usually hear about the failures of those you admire most, but rest assured that they have attempted lots of things that didn't work. They keep running the risk. They try and try until they get through. Then they tell you what they've learned.

In innovative churches I consistently find a senior pastor who keeps trying to discover what works. People who achieve breakthroughs in ministry don't allow setbacks to discourage them to the point of quitting.

Several of the most significant turning points in my life came because of huge failures on my part. For a person like me who has been very success oriented, it's not easy to face my own failures privately, let alone put them on display publicly. Yet I've learned that failure can evolve into my

—blessing in disguise,

—doorway to new opportunity,

—teacher of priceless lessons,

—enricher of personality,

—Pathway to a richer fellowship with God, and

—stepping-stone to truer success.

Sooner or later the "villain of letdown" robs everyone. My prayerful intention is that by addressing this topic, many readers will face up to their failures and with God's help experience personal growth.

Life-changing lessons I learned from failure. Almost every major personality profiled in the Bible seems to have experienced personal failure or to have come out of a scenario of failure. Yet God used each of them mightily! One cannot read the Bible with an open mind without seeing that God does not turn His back on people who have failed, but rather forgives them, strengthens them, and uses them to do wonderful things in the Kingdom. Classic examples include Moses, Samson, Jonah, David, Mark, Peter, and the other disciples. If God used these great saints of old after they failed, don't you believe He can still do something marvelous with you today—in spite of your failures?

Failure can even emerge as a good thing if it motivates us to move ahead to something better. I have come to love and live by the phrase popularized by my friend Dr. Robert Schuller, founder of the Crystal Cathedral, Garden Grove, California. He said, "I would rather attempt something great and fail than attempt nothing and succeed."

Because of these words, I ran the risk of failure by starting New Hope Community Church, Portland, Oregon, without any people or funds. To this day, more than 25 years later, I am so glad I didn't surrender to my past failings or very real fears of being unsuccessful.

God enabled me to overcome some big obstacles over the course of my adult life, both in previous pastorates and at New Hope:

Let love be your greatest aim."
—*(1 Cor. 14:1, TLB)*

1. Wrong priorities. One of my earliest failures was to put my goals and work as a minister in the church ahead of my family. For years I lived, despite the best intentions, with mixed-up priorities. I thought I did right by putting the church first in everything, while all the time neglecting my wife and children.

One day I read *The Living Bible,* and these words grabbed my heart: "Let love be your greatest aim" (1 Cor. 14:1, TLB). This concept literally turned my life right side up with change. I realized that people and relationships, starting with my family, must be more important than programs. Ever since that discovery, I have wanted a reputation for spreading the kind of love that begins at home with members of my family and then extends to the other people with whom I share the closest relationships.

2. Workaholism. As a workaholic, even when attending a party given by the young couples in our church, I would never let down, relax, and enjoy myself. I would always work, plot, plan, and get someone off to the side and sell them on a new idea or program that I wanted to develop.

God has since taught me that I can please Him by turning off the work completely and by fully enjoying times of play. As the ancient preacher put it, "There is a right time for everything: . . . a time to plant; . . . and a time to laugh" (Eccles. 3:1-4, TLB). What a transforming realization to discover that God loved me just as fully when I laughed and played as when I focused on church work!

3. Poor listening skills. In the past my preoccupation with what I planned to say or do next kept me from carefully hearing what others tried to communicate.

This correction didn't come easily. First I had to learn to stop thinking about what I needed to say next while someone else talked. Then I had to develop better skills at concentrating on the other person. I knew I had made progress when a staff member who had known me for years said, "Dale, I really appreciate what a good listener you have become." That was a very meaningful compliment.

4. Not validating my spouse's feelings. When my wife, Margi, feels hurt or upset, I have learned to hold her, to listen, and to validate her feelings as being OK and very important to me. Sometimes I still have to bite my tongue and resist the old temptation to correct or give immediate advice. I have also learned that part of caring for my wife and children involves keeping the home in good repair. In the past I would walk in and out of our broken screen door for days and never see it, even though it had been called to my attention again and again.

5. Not working at my marriage. I have learned that I must work at marriage to keep the relationship growing. I used to give so much of myself emotionally to other people that I had nothing left for meeting my mate's emotional needs. Most ministers and their spouses would agree that they have more difficulties getting along with each other on Monday than any other day of the week. Why? Because you have two emotionally drained people, each looking to the other for a lift, yet neither having anything left to give.

6. Judging other people. I have learned through my own failures to leave the judging to God. As Scripture warns, "Do not take revenge, my friends, but leave room for God's wrath, for it is written: 'It is mine to avenge; I will repay,' says the Lord. On the contrary: 'If your enemy is hungry, feed him; if he is thirsty, give him something to drink. In doing this, you will heap burning coals on his head.' Do not be overcome by evil, but overcome evil with good" (Rom. 12:19-21). My job is to keep on loving and believing in people in spite of their failures.

7. Insensitivity. In the past I wasn't as compassionate with hurting people as I should have been. God has taught me to show them the compassion and love of Jesus as I "rejoice with those who rejoice; [and] mourn with those who mourn" (Rom. 12:15).

8. Blindness to the "beams" in my eye. For years I was oblivious to my own weak spots and failures. I have since realized that the day I stop learning, I stop growing. With God's help I have changed, I am changing, and I will continue to change for the better. Learning from failures makes my motto, "The best is yet to come," a reality in my life.

How to feel like somebody again. I have never seen a man or woman able to live well with success who had not first traveled through the fires and storms of failure. Failure keeps people remembering, after they achieve the breakthroughs they seek, how other people hurt and feel. Truly successful individuals share the victory with others and help all those who have failed to also experience the joys of success.

God never sees you as a failure until you give up and quit trying. Someone has said, "A winner never quits, and a quitter never wins." We serve a God of love, hope, and bright tomorrows.

Claim the promises of God's Word: "Praise the LORD, O my soul, and forget not all his benefits—who forgives all your sins and heals all your diseases" (Ps. 103:2-3). Never allow yesterday's failures to wipe out the possibilities of tomorrow's successes.

▪4▪

CHOOSING ADVENTURE OVER STATUS QUO

Elmer Towns

Change the fabric of your own soul and
your own visions, and you change all.
—Vachel

To stimulate and expand my thinking about the adventuresome use of transition, I reread some of the underlined sections in several secular leadership books. In those sources I found lots of discussion on change as a positive, useful force for business leaders. I immediately saw the crossover to the church—how transitioning can be a positive force for ministry.

Cutting-edge church leaders have adopted "transitioning" as a term to describe change as an adventuresome opportunity. The word is used to describe a positive, purposeful process. Thus, transitioning in the church refers to ways change can be used to renew a congregation or to make it more relevant to the spiritual needs of contemporary people, both inside and outside the church. Usually, it represents change intentionally instituted by a leader or group of leaders to make the church more effective in fulfilling its mission. So for our purposes in this chapter, transitioning means positive and beneficial use of change.

The following basic assumptions from secular organizations can work well in spiritual organisms, such as a local church. Though these eight foundation ideas may present brand-new ways of thinking for many churches and leaders, I propose that each concept be carefully considered as part of a positive transitional environment for any church.

- **Change or die.** Everything is in a state of flux and change. The choice is not to stay the same and live, for to stay the same is to die.

- **Risk of not changing.** Refusing to change is often a bigger risk than changing, but many do not realize it. Complacency in a church can be more harmful than any problem change might cause.

- **Transition as normal.** Change should be built into the thinking of a congregation as the norm rather than something they are forced to do. If a leader can communicate that message, then negative, fearful resistance to change in the church might be nearly eliminated.

- **Three-year trial.** Every organization needs to be evaluated fairly often. Secular management specialist Peter Drucker thinks an organization should be put on trial for its life every three or four years—every process, policy, methodology, and service. Think what that would do to many churches.

- **Culture and environment.** Consider the environment when making a transition. Try to understand the kind of people you want to win. Who are they? Where do they live? How do they think? For the church that means it must always be aware of the culture in which ministry is done. Former President Jimmy Carter put it this way: "We must adjust to changing times and still hold to unchanging principles." The issue is to always be willing to change methods while keeping the message changeless.

- **Healthy churches.** Change should be viewed as a positive indicator of health and growth. Nobody expects a child to be the same at 4 as he will be at 14 or 40 or 64. George Gardner's words apply to the church: "I think that all human systems require continuous renewal. They rigidify. They get stiff in the joints. They forget what they cared about. The forces against it are nostalgia and the enormous appeal of having things the way they have always been, appeals to the supposedly happy past. But we've got to move on." If left alone too long, any church becomes rigid, self-serving, and stuck in status quo.

- **Small steps first.** Change is more easily accomplished in incremental steps than in catastrophic decisions that make everyone nervous. Each success builds confidence and trust for acceptance of future transitions.

• **Seasons of change.** Churches, like healthy human beings, experience periods of transitioning and tradition, stress and then calm, growth and then stabilizing gains, continuity and crises, hunger and plenty. The secret is to recognize these realities and move forward at the best possible time but at the same time not to be overly concerned with fall seasons and stretches of winter of the spirit.

Many of the ideas in this chapter started with a conversation with John Maxwell some years ago. John and I first met in Davenport, Iowa, at the Sunnyside Temple at a three-day conference for pastors where Dr. Robert Schuller and I were the speakers. I had come in the previous night, preached, and done the assigned workshops, and I was finished. I was eating lunch by myself at the Howard Johnson's Motel. I looked across the aisle, and there was a young preacher about 25 years old. It was John Maxwell. I asked if he was at the conference and invited him to eat with me. I told him I was going to Chicago to another conference and asked him to go with me. We flew to Chicago, spent time together, and have been friends ever since.

My God-assigned ministry has been to train young people for Christian service, so I have been teaching in Bible colleges and seminaries all my life. That is what God called me to do—to pass on the ministry concepts and experiences to the next generation. My relationship with John has been a unique combination of learning as much as teaching. To be near John Maxwell is to be stretched to be a great Christian leader for God. John believes in transitioning the church to the greatest possible effectiveness. By his modeling, pastoring, writing, organizing, and resourcing, he has impacted Evangelical Christianity as much as any one person. He makes change, innovation, and transitioning sound essential and doable.

WHAT ARE THE MOST DIFFICULT THINGS TO CHANGE

Let's consider seven difficult changes. Try using this list as a discussion starter with your lay leaders. Ask each one to rate the list and then compare scores. Their answers will give you many clues about transitioning in your setting.

1. Change the doctrinal statement. I did that in the second church I served because we only had about eight simple sentences and we made it much more complete. It was easy to get a unanimous vote because we amplified it rather than changed it.

2. Change the name of the church. The second church I pastored was Nomas Street Chapel, and we changed the name to Faith Bible Church. A name change is easier when the need is obvious but difficult if the old name carries emotional warmth. Caution should also be used in selecting a new name to be sure it is accurate. The term "Bible church" where little of the Bible is preached may create a false impression. "Community" as part of a name change for a church detached from its community may not be wise.

If you tamper with the 11 A.M. service and don't do it right, it will be new résumé time for you as pastor.

3. Change the location of the church. The intensity of this difficulty is determined by the stated and real reasons for moving.

4. Replace a board member. That can be easy, difficult, or terminal—meaning termination of the pastor. When forced to choose sides, lay leaders will most naturally choose the side of the board member. Never forget that laypeople often have long-term relationships that the pastor can cultivate, recognize, and appreciate but will find difficult to undermine or destroy.

5. Change a staff member. If you hire someone for the wrong reason, you will have to change that staff member. By the nature of specialized ministries, staff people have significant groups who believe in them. For example, terminating a music minister without considering the views of the choir has split hundreds of churches.

6. Change to add another worship service. When you "mess" with 11 A.M., you are touching the most untouchable meeting time a church has. If you tamper with the 11 A.M. service and don't do it right, it will be new résumé time for you as pastor.

7. You want to cancel the evening service. One of the reasons why this change is so different is because it is often viewed as spiritual retrenchment, which it often is. Thus this change has to describe what will take its place. Also, it should be recognized that some of the most faithful people in the church attend this service.

I suggest you work through this list with your decision makers. Give them a simple quiz, and then discuss the results. New insights will jump out of the discussion, and you will gain a considerable new understanding of how your leaders think and how they process new ideas.

THE CHANGE PROCESS IN A LOCAL CONGREGATION

Just as a human being cannot grow without change, a church does not grow without change. Until you change, you cannot grow. Until your organization changes, it cannot grow. Not all change is growth, but no growth ever happens without some change.

The reasons for the need to change are the future is not going to be like the past and the future will not be like what anyone expects. Not long ago on public television there was a broadcast from the '50s telling what life was going to be like in the '90s. They talked in terms of things that were almost laughable. They said gasoline is going to be cheap. They said electricity was going to be inexpensive because of nuclear power. They talked about the things that were going to happen but didn't. TV was to replace books, and computers were to make us a paperless society.

The rate of change in the future will be exponential. You will see things happen and change and explode. Some of us grew up in the day of 1 channel, 3 channels, 13 channels, 36 channels, 99 channels; and DVDs are coming like a fast train. Donald Nelson, though likely not speaking about the church, offers us helpful advice:

> We must drop the idea that change comes slowly. It does ordinarily—in part because we think it does. Today changes must come fast; and we must adjust our mental habits, so that we can accept comfortably the idea of stop-

ping one thing and beginning another overnight. We must discard the idea that past routine, past ways of doing things, are probably the best ways. On the contrary, we must assume that there is probably a better way to do almost everything. We must stop assuming that a thing which has never been done before probably cannot be done at all.

WHY PEOPLE RESIST CHANGE

Resistance to change is more often due to fear and confusion than lack of spiritual commitment. Think how leaders make fearful people feel when they accuse them of spiritual shallowness or low commitment. The following are some of the reasons people resist change:

1. Misunderstanding. Some people are so frightened they cannot process information on why change is needed or useful. People oppose change if they don't understand it. They oppose new Bible versions, new music, and new liturgy. Good people, like everyone else, resist what they do not understand.

2. Lack of ownership. They resist it if they are not included in making the plan. In the instance of going to two services, the pastor should not make the decision, but create and manage lay leaders' and congregants' ownership of the decision. A good way to do it is to chop a decision into about six small parts. The idea is to bring your leaders and members through several small decisions before they are faced with one big decision. For example, when you are talking about going to multiple worship services, you ask your people, "If we have the same kind of worship service at 6 P.M. Saturday and 8:30 A.M. and 11 A.M. Sunday, when would you like to come?" Have them express their preferences by a show of hands. In this effort, you educate leaders that there are a number of individuals in your church who would attend at a different time. You allow the church to speak to the church while you merely manage their decision.

Then come back in two to three weeks and pass out cards for them to express their preferences. Even though you lead people in making a decision, you do not stake your ministry on a second worship service, because if it fails, you go down with it. Before the vote, bring in a video of a contemporary worship service from a church you especially like. Have the people look at it and discuss it. Ask, "Could we do that?" Then consider "why we could, why we could not," and then lead the people to make the vote. This is done by your beginning to talk about reaching more people—the passion of why your church should add a worship service. This process suggests pastoring in the future is not making decisions but managing decisions.

You continue encouraging and managing a decision by talking about the problems ahead of time. Then pass out the opinion cards again. This third time, ask if another service was available, would they commit to attend for six consecutive Sundays. Suggest they start Palm Sunday and attend an additional worship service until the first week of May. Try this experiment. Many will buy into an experiment.

3. **Habit patterns are hard to break.** It may be hard to get people to come to an early service, but many pastors find after five years it is hard to get anyone to leave the early service. The pattern I discovered is that if you go to an early service and later drop it, those people who have become acclimated to the early service will transfer to another church instead of returning to the 11 A.M. service.

4. **The threat of loss.** Transitions often mean someone loses something that is valuable to him or her. A few years ago our church added a praise band—drums, horns, saxophone—and we lost five families. My dentist left the church and told us why: "I used to dance to that type of music before I was a Christian. Now I am not going to worship God to it."

5. **Negative attitude toward change.** This is what I call the set-in-my-ways attitude. The old story is told about the aging deacon to whom a younger leader said, "I bet you've seen a lot of changes in the church since you were a little boy." The gruff old man replied, "Yes, and I've been against every one of them." Some people have been so stressed by changes at work, home, and church that they want change kept out of the church. But it can't be done.

6. **Lack of trust for pastor.** They may think you do not know what you're doing. They may wonder if you plan to stay awhile. They may not know whether you can raise money for the change. If they don't believe in you, they won't follow you.

7. **Tradition.** They have never done it this way before. Traditions are a part of everyone's life. Traditions usually kick in when persons feel overstressed or have experienced a high level of ambiguity in other areas of their lives.

THE INGREDIENTS FOR EFFECTIVE TRANSITIONS

1. **Be open to change yourself.** The easiest way for you to lead your church into praise music is for you to be open to praise music. In transition seasons in a local church, all eyes will be on the leader. Expect it.

very time a leader produces a significant victory in the church, people will gladly follow through additional innovations.

2. **Create an atmosphere of trust.** When I interviewed Dr. Paul Walker for my book on 10 innovative churches, he said, "When a pastor has been in a church a long time and the people trust the pastor, he has led through innovations before, they will trust him to lead through innovations again." Give the congregation lots of opportunities to trust you. Be faithful, loyal, dependable, and consistent. Trust requires giving people a reason why the change is good for them.

3. **Build off of previous track record.** Your track record is a key ingredient to getting something changed. Every time a leader produces a significant victory in the church, people will gladly follow through additional innovations. It is like having a bank account from which to draw emotional and spiritual capital. The pastor who has grown the church, built an impressive new building, and demonstrated love for people will be viewed as trustworthy. This is not something to place on a to-do list but a way of life.

4. **Admit mistakes.** Every effective leader makes many mistakes, and the people know it. Love, acceptance, and even devotion follow a leader who can say, "I goofed. Please forgive me." You don't have to always be right. You just have to be a respected human being who is seeking to be like Christ.

5. Ask yourself three questions to see if the change is worthwhile:
  A. Is this idea God's or mine?
  B. Am I willing to pay the price in money, free time, professional time, and energy?
  C. Who will you lose?

6. Get the main person involved. This is the one individual in the church who is essential to make the transition happen. You must give this person the vision for the change. He or she must see it and believe it.

I learned this principle almost by accident. I was 19 years old and pastoring my first church—Westminster Presbyterian Church in Savannah, Georgia. It was a large old wooden church located in a declining neighborhood of large Victorian houses that had been converted into apartments. The church had been closed, but I opened it. As I was visiting in the neighborhood, a lady said to me, "I wouldn't come to your church. It looks like it's about to fall down. The paint is all puckered and falling off. The front porch has rotten boards. Your church doesn't need revival. What it really needs is a coat of paint."

That did something inside me. So the next Sunday, while I was leading the singing for Sunday School, I said, "We ought to paint the church." Nobody moved. When they didn't respond, I challenged them for noninvolvement.

As I taught the junior boys' class, I stuck a blue piece of chalk in my coat pocket. In the morning service, I held up the blue chalk to say, "See this piece of chalk? This Saturday, with the help of this piece of chalk, we are going to paint the whole church in one day." I stood silently for impact. Then I said, "This church needs paint so bad I'm going to go draw a blue line with this chalk at 10-foot intervals. Then I'm going to write Miller on the first section."

"Mr. Miller, can you and your family paint that 10-foot section?" He quickly said "Yes!" Several others agreed to paint 10-foot sections.

Then Mr. Seckinger, the chairman of the elders since Noah, said, "We don't have enough ladders around here." So he started asking people out loud if they had ladders. He took their names down.

Mr. Strickland, another elder, asked where the paint was coming from. I had no idea. So Mr. Strickland, who was a plumbing contractor, said he would get the paint and brushes. Soon it seemed as if everyone in the congregation was talking at the same time. I just listened as the people planned to paint the whole church in a single day.

Though the idea was brilliant, I did not have a clue as to what I was doing. I stumbled into this idea of leadership. When the parishioners bought into my vision of painting the church, they bought into my leadership. When the main man, Mr. Seckinger, bought into the vision, we got the job done.

When Saturday arrived, we painted from about 7:00 till 12:30. Approximately 80 people turned out to help. We had more unsaved people painting the church than had ever attended to hear me preach. People showed up, and we put them to work.

In the middle of the day, Mr. Seckinger said, "You know, if we're going to paint the outside, we ought to do something about the inside." He said the old rugs smelled bad, so he and I ripped them out. Then he said something I have never forgotten: "It's easier to get forgiveness than to get permission." We ripped rugs out, but we didn't take them outside until we had them all up.

The principle worked. In my next pastorate, we painted the whole church in a day. When I became a college president, we painted the whole college in one day. It's amazing what you can do when you get everybody to work together.

7. **Know your decision makers well.** You must have their influence to back what you are doing. You must know where they stand—positive or negative—to a proposed change. You need to know how much money they give and what they do in the way of service. John Maxwell is right when he says you are paid to know your board. It is highly advisable to never bring an issue to an official vote until you know how every decision maker will vote. You never get to be their leader just by standing up and saying, "Follow me" or "Vote my way." You have to lead them spiritually before you can lead them organizationally.

8. **Include those who are most affected by the change. Look for positive involvement.** Ask for input. Appeal to their in-

terests. Ask how they feel about the proposed change. Remember, these are the people who are most likely the ones to make the transitions work.

For example, a pastor of a great 4,000-member church decided to close down the evening service. Since less than 400 were coming back to church on Sunday night—about 10 percent of the membership—it was easy for him to conclude that there was not enough interest in continuing the service. The evening service met in a sanctuary that seated 3,000! So it seemed like a waste of energy and staff time to come.

But his proposal to close the service started a blazing firestorm of negative response. The reactions were what you might expect if you were voting to change a church's doctrinal stand. It caused such a flap that the decision group voted to continue with the evening service. The problem was that the 400 had not been consulted. And by their attendance they were already voting that they thought the evening service had value and significance for them.

The psator and decision makers were using their best judgment when they considered closing the evening service. They had the statistics and the low attendance on their side, but they failed to consult the people who were the most involved. Wisely, as a response to the negative reaction, the church continued its evening service but has added other church activities meeting at the same time. And the attendance has grown.

S *ometimes, the wise leader waits for a better day.*

Into this mix must be added the tension of giving people what they want and what they need. Bill Hybels explains that "we design programs based around what people want thinly disguised to give them what they really need." This issue is especially critical in developing discipling areas of ministry.

9. Give careful attention to timing. Often the Lord provides a window of opportunity for accomplishing a great achievement for Him. Decisions are important, but the time of making a decision is fully as important as the decision itself. You can have the right decision and the wrong timing, and the decision does not fly. Sometimes the wise leader waits for a better day. Sometimes a lot of informal discussion and on-site training is needed before a decision can be made authentically. Sometimes as you think and pray about a decision, it could be that the timing is not right and that God will help you find the best time.

Sometimes the wise thing is to plant the seed and wait for it to grow. The wrong decision at the wrong time is a disaster. The right decision at the wrong time is also unacceptable. The right decision at the right time leads to success. Timing is an important part of the decision-making process, and many lay leaders are clueless on this issue.

EFFECTIVE TRANSITIONING MEANS MAKING GOOD DECISIONS

A leader carries the obligation to help the church he or she serves make the right decisions at the right time. Transitioning from what was to what can be means that the one who leads must finally take the people through a series of decisions to get to the desired outcome. By the nature of the ministry, every pastor is deciding moment by moment what kind of pastor to be, what kind of church to serve, and what is the measure of commitment to be made to see the Kingdom advance in that setting. A pastor does not have the luxury of playing it safe for long if his or her life is to count and the church is to thrive. Those being led trust the pastor to lead, and leading is making decisions, helping others make decisions, and transitioning the church to a greater tomorrow.

If I could say anything to all of you about how to become better pastors, greater leaders, more effective men and women of God, I would say learn how to make decisions on a timely basis. Many times I have gotten alone with God and started writing all the facts on a legal pad. I begin to look at all the information. I consider every option I can imagine. I try to write down everything I can do.

Then I make a list of possible decisions. The right decision, the almost-right decision, the stupid decision, and the unattainable decision. I exhaust my thinking.

Decision making is not usually about finding something new you do not already know. Nor is it about finding a panacea. It is really choosing among all the alternatives and options.

Always remember, no transition happens without a decision on someone's part. And no decision is always a decision not to act, and it leads to status quo and no achievement.

Let us make our decisions and lead our transitions with the awareness that shines and speaks through the prayer of South American priest Dom Helder Camara:

Every step I take
reminds me
That, wherever I am going,
I am always on the march to eternity.

"5"

CHANGE AFTER A MUCH-LOVED PREDECESSOR

Mike Breaux

Everyone benefits by a success transition:
the incumbent, the board, the successor,
the ministry and the Kingdom.
—Wallace Erickson (former CEO of Compassion Inc.)

Since I grew up in the town where I'm now pastoring, I know a lot about the culture there. I never thought I would put that understanding to work by pastoring there.

SURPRISING TRANSITIONS GOD BROUGHT TO MY MINISTRY

I went to school in Illinois and spent 12 years in youth ministry before coming back to central Kentucky to pastor my first church in Harrodsburg. That chapter of my life was really refreshing. The Spirit was moving. Many people came to know Christ. I remember telling my wife, "We are going to have grandkids here. I mean I love this church! I am never going to leave this church."

From Harrodsburg to Las Vegas. Then came God's first surprising intervention. I received a call from Las Vegas, Nevada, and the caller said, "We want you to come plant a new church out here."

I responded, "Excuse me? Now where did you say?"

He said, "Vegas."

I said, "Hang on a second. Do I understand that you want me to come to Las Vegas to plant a church?"

I remember thinking that's an oxymoron—Vegas-church. That did not compute in my brain. I started thinking, "What's a church going to be like in Vegas? Are you going to have tithe machines in the lobby? Or bikini-clad girls announcing hymn numbers across the platform? Or maybe Wayne Newton would become an elder?"

We began to realize that God was calling us to go. So we packed up and moved to Las Vegas to plant a new church. I had never planted a church. The sponsoring congregations had never planted a church. But they said with gusto, "Let's try it. God has given us a vision. Let's just launch out and do this." So we did. And God blessed our efforts.

This church plant turned out to be an awesome experience of effectiveness and blessing. We started in the Greater Las Vegas YMCA, where we set up chairs in the gym and used racquetball courts as kids' classrooms. It was just crazy every Sunday. But God made it happen, so in two years the church grew to an attendance of 1,500 people.

It was a God event. He just said, "Boom! I am going to use you to plant a church!" And He did it through us. In the process, this young church felt like a 6'4" toddler stomping around Las Vegas. It was hard but gratifying. It was so much fun. Nobody even said "We've never done it like that," because we as a church had never done much of anything before. We had no homesteader-type members, no history, no traditions, no power brokers. We tried new things all the time. It was exciting, and I said to my wife, "You know what? We're going to have grandkids here." I have learned not to say that anymore.

From Vegas to central Kentucky. Now for a second surprise: In the middle of the Vegas adventure, I received a call to lead a men's retreat in central Kentucky. I thought it would be an opportunity to see my extended family in Kentucky. It sounded good—speak at this men's retreat, play a little golf, and relax. Then I would go back to Canyon Ridge in Las Vegas to launch our capital stewardship campaign to fund our first building.

That's exactly what I intended to do. But just before I left

Las Vegas for central Kentucky, I got a phone call from the pastor of Southland Christian Church, Wayne Smith. He said, "My knee hurts so I can't stand up to preach this week. Since you are going to be in town, would you mind filling in for me?"

I replied jovially, "Sure. Have sermon, will travel. I will be glad to preach for you."

So I led the men's retreat and spoke in the Sunday morning service at Southland as I had been requested to do. The service was powerful and scary—something indescribable I cannot explain happened. I knew something was happening but did not want to even consider what all this meant.

People were saying that guy who preached today is going to be our new preacher. I thought, "New preacher—what are you talking about?"

That afternoon, Wayne Smith phoned and said, "I listened to you on the radio today, and it couldn't be more clear if God had sat down next to me on my couch. God said I am supposed to retire and you're the guy to replace me."

Rain on my golf plans. I told Wayne, "What! No, I'm not! I came here to preach and to play a little golf, and that's it! Then get out of town. Go home!"

It rained every day. I could not play one hole of golf. Lay leaders wanted to meet with me. Every day they would get little groups together and talk to me about the possibility of my coming as pastor.

Wayne told them, "I'm done—it's time for me to retire. Go get him. I am finished. I really am ready to retire. Right now."

It was unbelievable how God confirmed my call to Southland during those initial conversations. Here is a church that, after 40 years of being led by one pastor, had an extensive 10-step calling process they had developed to be used whenever Smith retired. They were going to search the country and consider as many résumés as possible—perhaps 100 or more.

However, as our conversation continued and our relationship developed, they threw their well-defined procedures in the trash and said, "God is moving here."

Then they initiated an informal conversation with this invitation: "Wednesday night before you leave, we are having a little get-together. Would you like to come?"

I said, "Sure, I'll come."

I expected a little informal get-together. In reality, it was a quickly, quietly called interview. I showed up and discovered 20 guys were sitting around a conference table waiting to talk with me. I was glad I did not wear shorts and a T-shirt—as I often do, especially on vacation. I sat down at a little space they had reserved for me at the table. They were serious and resolute. They had to put together a committee in a span of three days and were asking me if I wanted to be their pastor. And they asked me a lot of questions.

In the course of the two days, I jotted down a top-10 list of reasons why they would not want to call me as pastor. I was completely transparent and said, "I have to be in a church that is ready to do relevant things. I am really different. I am so different that you might see me at the mall with my hat on backward and a pair of baggy basketball shorts on. You might be embarrassed to say that's our preacher. That's who I am."

God, why would You pull me out of a place that is so cutting edge and move me to a place where somebody is going to yell at me for not singing their songs anymore?

After that speech I thought I was off the hook. But nothing slowed the process down. After the meeting they handed me a note that said, "We have exhausted our search until we have your decision." I left Lexington and went back to Las Vegas. My wife picked me up at the airport to drive me to a "pastor's appreciation dinner." I felt as if I had been having an affair in Kentucky. My Las Vegas folks were telling me how much they loved me and how they wouldn't have known Christ without me. All the while I am thinking, "If you only knew what I have been doing for the last three days."

In a short while, the Southland Church sent five guys out to Vegas just to make sure. They observed our service, and I thought, "They will absolutely hate it. There will be no way they will call me, and I won't have to make a decision." We were kicking off our capital stewardship campaign that day. We had all the people packed in the gym. We had video. We had a band. We had a drama. I told myself these guys will see it and say, "Oh, we didn't know this. No, he's not coming."

But the Spirit of God convicted their hearts—and mine too. They cried in the parking lot. They later called me and said, "We really want you to come. We think God is moving here and though our hearts break for Canyon Ridge, we believe that God is leading in all this.

From cutting edge to traditional competence. I was thinking, "God, why would You pull me out of a place that is so cutting edge and move me to a place where somebody is going to yell at me for not singing their songs anymore? I am not sure I need this in my life right now."

God said, "But I need you to make this move." I wrestled with God for a long time.

I remember sitting on a park bench and coming down to the defining moment and thinking, "Am I going or am I not?" With just me and God and my prayer journal, I started crying. It was almost as if God was saying to me, "You know the problem. You don't want to leave this church because you think it is *your* church. But I planted this church. And I will take care of it. I want you to go. Be strong and courageous."

So with that, I got up, wiped my eyes, closed my prayer journal, and told Debbie we were moving. She said, "What? Last night you said we were staying." I said, "I lied! I knew then that we were supposed to move to Kentucky. I just couldn't let go!"

The most courageous but difficult thing I have ever done is to stand up the next week and say, "I have to tell you something before we launch into this building program. You're going to reach this valley for Christ, but without me." I did not understand it, and neither did they. It was tough to leave. And it still pains me to think about it.

The Las Vegas church is doing amazingly well. They just moved into a new building; more than 3,500 people now attend Canyon Ridge. It is just now an eight-year-old church.

Pastor Wayne Smith's commitment to smooth transition. Now my focus was directed to Kentucky. Since I grew up in this area, I knew Wayne Smith, minister of Southland Christian Church. He was a legend in his own time as the faithful pastor

I feel like Barney Fife checking in for Michael Jordan.

who lovingly served one church for 40 years. There is nobody like him. He is one of the funniest guys I know. He is compassionate. I went to his retirement party at Memorial Coliseum, where 7,000 people showed up. I sat there looking at all those people, and the master of ceremonies said, "Who here has ever had a visit from Wayne over the years in the hospital?" All these people stood up. "How many here have been to a funeral done by Wayne?" All these people stood up. "How many people have had fried chicken brought to their house by Wayne Smith?" All these people stood up. "How many people have been baptized by Wayne Smith?" All these people stood up.

I was sitting next to my teenage daughter, and I said, "You know what? I feel like Barney Fife checking in for Michael Jordan." I was really scared, and my daughter said, "Good, I am glad you feel that way, because you have to depend upon God if you are going to make this thing happen." So based on the wisdom of my teenage kid, I breathed a prayer, "OK, God, here we go."

The transition was greatly assisted by Wayne Smith's letter to the congregation that said this:

I've written my column in the *Voice* nearly every week for 40 years. This one is the most difficult—it is the last! It's been a great 40 years and a smooth transition. However, a successful start does not guarantee a quality finish. On the golf course or the Christian life, follow-through is essential. Permit me to share some thoughts that I call follow-through. If we are not spiritually mature with the following items, Mike's efficiency is hampered and my retirement will be less than I had hoped for.

He continued with this list:

1. Welcome change.
2. I am no longer your minister.
3. Embrace Mike and release Wayne.
4. Please don't call or visit me to complain.
5. Stay focused on others.
6. Stay committed to unity.

Wayne Smith prepared the people so well by reminding them that things would not stay the same. Things would change. What a gracious and wonderful assistance his letter was to my becoming the pastor at Southland after his long and loving years of service.

TWELVE STRATEGIES TO MAKE TRANSITIONS WORK EFFECTIVELY

Every pastor, except the church planter, feels the pressure that comes from following another pastor. Some do it with grace, and the church is strengthened. Others do it poorly, and nearly everyone is embarrassed or offended.

Comments with ambiguous meaning such as these can bug a new pastor:

"Pastor, you have big shoes to fill."

"Dr. Brown was the first pastor our family ever had."

"Rev. Smith loved to visit our home."

Sadly, the problem is usually in the pastor's head rather than in the people's remarks or intentions. In fact, most congregants want the new pastor to do well. Therefore, their observations are either meaningless small talk or poorly phrased words of intended encouragement.

In the months and years since Wayne Smith's retirement, I have discovered 12 strategies that helped make the transition work.

Communicate your vision. Make sure your vision is God's vision. When you are sure you have God's direction, you must communicate the vision again and again and again in conversation, publications, committee meetings, and sermons.

One of the first things I did was to say something like this: "I need to shoot straight with you right from the beginning. I am not interested in reshuffling the deck here. I mean for us to reach people who do not know Christ. That is the main motive for my ministry and the church's reason for being."

Right off I did a sermon series called "Do It Again, God!" I got the idea from the story of the elderly minister who couldn't preach any longer because he couldn't read his Bible since he had lost his eyesight. So he just put his hand on the Book of Acts and prayed, "Do it again, God; do it again!" Over and over in that series I preached that that's what we want to become—a biblically functioning community like Acts 2. In that seven-Sunday series, I preached on the core values of the Church and communicated what I believe God intended His Church to be.

My first sermon was titled "Signs"—remember that song from the '70s that said, "Signs, signs, everywhere signs . . ."? I did a little bit of that song, and then I talked about signs every church has hanging around. They may not be visibly hanging up, but every church has signs such as these:

"I Am Sorry—You Are the Wrong Color—You Don't Belong Here."

"I Am Sorry, but Change Your Past and Then You Can Come."

"Change Your Clothes and Then Come Back."

"Let's Be Honest—We Really Do Want Your Money."

I said there are three signs we need to have hanging in this church. The first is "Come As You Are." I took them to Rev. 22:17 where "the Spirit and the bride say, 'Come!' . . . whoever wishes, let him take the free gift." I talked about how we cannot be an exclusive club where you are expected to dress a certain way, drive a certain car, possess a certain amount of money, have a certain skin color, or live in a certain part of town. The right message is come as you are with all your baggage and your past. Come just as you are.

"Grace Happens" is the second sign. The grace of God is the most attractive thing in the world, and if we aren't preaching it, we are missing the good news of the gospel.

The third sign is "You Matter to God." That has become our unofficial slogan.

I wanted to share those three big ideas from the start. I wanted to communicate those biblical mandates from the pulpit, in writing, and through casual conversations. To make concepts like these a reality, a pastor must beat the "core-value drum" all the time.

Build on what God has done. Embrace the past with gratitude. The pastor before you did many things well. The people who helped him or her the most will help you if you give your predecessor credit and honor. I always try to remember that many great achievements happened before I arrived—in fact, that might be one of the important reasons why this current assignment challenges me.

The pastor I followed was a much-loved minister, and I try to stand on his shoulders and build on his sturdy work. I want people to know that Wayne Smith laid a tremendous foundation for our future. He sacrificed his life, his time, and his family. Beyond his work are the sacrifice and commitments of hundreds of people over many years to give us what we now have. I often say, "This is a great church, but it is becoming an even greater church. We are becoming more and more the type of church God wants us to be."

Be the predecessor's greatest fan. I made a decision that I was going to put my ego on the shelf and become Wayne Smith's biggest cheerleader. Refuse to say anything negative about the previous pastor. Give praise often. Write a note of appreciation. Make a phone call.

Quote him every now and then. Wayne had little trademark sentences such as, "If you wait till all the lights are green, you'll never go downtown." Or, "You gotta eat the biscuit while it's hot." He also had the most incredible laugh I have ever heard. So occasionally I will slip in a "Wayneism" and laugh as he did, and everybody will say, "Hey, Wayne's back."

Develop a feeling of genuine friendship with your predecessor. Keep in mind that in most cases, if the former pastor still wanted to be pastor of the church, he or she would never have resigned and left an opening for you.

Get control of your ego. Many pastors have fragile egos. Remember—not even God can please everybody. I know not everybody is going to like me. We made some significant methodology modifications, and new methods are where people usually go crazy.

Let me share two responses that represent only a small minority of our people.

So that you understand the irony of the responses, I must tell you what has happened in 5 years. It has been a God-thing—no other explanation. When a minister who is a much-loved legend leaves, many churches take a nosedive. But following this pastoral transition at Southland, immediately 2,000 more people started coming. Now, 4 years later, we are over 7,500. It has been mind-boggling as we have tried to figure out what to do with all these people. In the midst of all these people finding salvation, and the Holy Spirit moving through the church, I received letters like this.

Dear Brothers in Christ,

More and more, concern, frustration, and now developing anger has begun to surface among the Body of Christ. One can sense a spirit of strife, confusion, and misunderstanding moving in and through our midst. There is a perception that self-serving motives underpin the praise and worship music ministry. . . .We are receiving a lot of practical teaching, quality teaching that is based on the Word, a practical application of the Word if you will. Certainly this is good, but should practical application be a substitute for the preaching and teaching of the Word itself?

When that letter arrived, I was troubled. It was well written, organized—and it was about me. I wanted to quit, but I didn't. Letters, however, were not the extent of the resistance. Someone even orchestrated an informal protest meeting about three months after my coming to Southland, where they developed this list of complaints:

Services were no longer quiet and reverent.

Should be a Sunday night service.

Worship should be a place where you enter into the presence of God.

Church is no place for secular music.

We have lowered the church to the level of the unsaved.

We would prefer to evangelize the congregation rather than the community.

The Holy Spirit is no longer present.

Stained-glass windows are being covered too frequently.

A major problem seems to be that there is a platform full of ego-musicians.

Why is the rock-and-roll band on the stage?

What kind of dress code is there when we openly invite people to come as they are?

But what is the worst thing that is going to happen to a person who doesn't know Christ, who never connects with the Church?

None of this crowd should give up but stay and fight for their rights—this is their church.

From my perspective, the list is amazing, interesting, disturbing, amusing, and preposterous. Now many of those people have moved on to other churches. I still love them and deeply regret that the differences could not be healed, since I was their spiritual leader.

I had to evaluate this leaving-and-losing issue and the personal threats. So I asked myself, "What's the worst thing that can happen to a believer that doesn't like what's going on? He or she can go to another church. But what is the worst thing that is going to happen to a person who doesn't know Christ, who never connects with the Church? He or she is going to go to hell."

It is a no-brainer for me. Christ compels us to reach the unreached at the same time He calls us to make disciples and to care for the flock of God. Our ministry has a delicate balance of winning and developing and serving those who have never heard and those who have been Christians for years.

Don't take criticism personally. When you internalize censure, the critic steals your sleep and causes ulcers, stress, and chest pains.

Of course, it is always advisable to consider the source of criticism and the motive of the one who criticizes. Criticism is like cholesterol—some good and some not so good. The good kind helps us improve and find better ways of doing ministry.

Some criticisms should be ignored. Sometimes the church's

best interest is served when the leader acts as if nothing has been uttered. Criticism may be mere human nature reacting in fear to change. Sometimes criticism has malicious intent. Some criticism, however, is merely social interaction where people talk to fill up the stillness.

When I was taking heat in the last few months, a friend gave me that word from Joshua—"Be strong and courageous" (1:6). Another friend pulled me aside and reminded me about the Old Testament incident (see 2 Sam. 16) when David was forced to leave Jerusalem because of his son's rebellion. This little guy named Shimei threw rocks at David and cursed him. David's general asked, "Want me to cut his head off?" David responded, "No, may the Lord teach me through his cursing."

Criticism is sometimes rooted in a sense of loss. Acknowledge and help people grieve the loss of their former pastor. Many at our church went through a grief process when Wayne left. It should be expected and certainly not ignored. I mean 40 years— a great friend, a wonderful pastor, and all of a sudden this new leader is here and these new people are coming. The people who had been around for a while lost their preacher, their parking places, their pews, and even their hymnbooks.

It was as if they had lost about everything at church. So gather a bunch of people together, put your arms around them, and say, "You know, we're going to get through this; we really are. God is going to take us through this transition."

Maintain a Barnabas file. Develop a file of letters of positive comments. Think how good these letters will sound to you on a rainy day. To be candid, I received a stack of negative letters and those dreaded pew rack comment cards at the start of my ministry at Southland Church. To balance the scales, I also received many positive, affirming letters. So when things are not going well or I receive a negative letter, I read through letters in my Barnabas file. That helps me find balance.

This one provided a lift:

> We haven't met yet, but I just had to send you this note. Last Sunday's worship service and the encounter services are fantastic. The things the Holy Spirit is doing at Southland are wonderful. I know whatever the topic in your

preaching, it will be delivered with honesty, genuine concern, plenty of love, no condemnation, lots of humor, and a bounty of Scripture to back up the message. You are not shying away from uncomfortable or formidable biblical truths, yet wrapping them in a cloak of love and forgiveness. You offer real, practical biblical solutions, challenges, and suggestions. Best of all, you offer hope.

Another recent letter read like this: "I can't express how much this ministry has changed my life. Two months ago, my life was in total chaos. I was addicted to methamphetamines. I also was abusing alcohol, all the while denying my problems to friends and family. My remorse was of epic proportion, and my head was a mess." Then after talking about being desperate and suicidal, she ends the letter, "When I came to church, I felt this unconditional wave of love wash over me, and I felt like I had come out of hell."

Yea, God! Save the positive letters. They will encourage and motivate you when your spirit sags and your energy seems depleted.

This shared vision and ongoing caring relationship with key leaders has been a significant factor in our transition and growth.

Build relationships with key leaders. Strong relationships with key leaders help ripple your vision across the entire congregation.

Since key leaders and/or the most effective influencers are not always elected to positions of authority and trust, you may need help determining who they are. I asked staff members, "If you started a new church out of our congregation, which 5 persons would you pick as leaders?" I asked every staff person to independently list 5.

Out of those combined lists, I chose 10 persons I would pour my life into and challenge to help me carry out the vision. I went to each one and said, "I need you. We can't make this dream happen unless we team up. You have been identified as somebody who is a leader, and I need you on the team."

This shared vision and ongoing caring relationship with key leaders has been a significant factor in our transition and growth. They help transform the vision into reality. And what a joy comes to me as I watch these individuals grow into strong, effective Christian leaders.

Build relationships with staff. When a new leader comes, it is natural to have some staff defection.

Such a loss did not happen at Southland Church. We have 120 people on staff, and only 1 left during the transition. We have developed great camaraderie from having fun together, hanging out together, sharing dreams together, and thinking outside the box together. If the bottom line of a staff member's purpose is to share the senior pastor's dream with the congregation and to be an extension of his or her ministry to the people of God, the staff member must know the pastor well and interact with him or her often.

Surround yourself with a small group. In my ministerial training I was taught that when you lead in ministry, you cannot be close to anybody. But that assumption needs to be rethought. Paul had Timothy, and Silas had Barnabas. I need people like that in my life. As a result, when I first came to Southland Church, I looked for men I could identify as having the potential to be my close friends.

Here's a significant principle for me. If I expect everyone in our church to be in a small group, I have to be in one too. I need one. I need friends to help overcome my loneliness and to help me have a reality check on my work for God. So surround yourself with a small group to whom you make yourself accountable. Such a group offers the pastor an opportunity to understand how the gospel works in the workplace.

Cultivate friendships with intercessors. At our church each staff member has five prayer partners who pray for him or her every day. It is comforting to know someone is talking to God about you every single day.

Give intentional priority to your family. When moving into a new community, the pastor's family goes through transitions that may be more traumatic than the minister faces. You have immediate contacts—people who need and affirm you—but your family often feels like strangers in the church as well as newcomers to the community and school. And the children and spouse are objects of comparison because they are not like the previous pastor's family.

Put your family at the top of your priority list, and intentionally make time for them in your calendar. Since the family was God's idea at creation, then pastors do themselves, their families, and their congregations a needed service in making them VIPs in their priorities. They sacrifice to see your dreams of ministry come true, so they need you and you need them.

When I first arrived, I took a lot of shots. People were saying, "Change. We're overdosing on change." During that period, I tended to go home, plop in the recliner, eat Doritos, and complain, "Oh-h-h, this is so hard. I don't know why we moved here." While I was having my pity party, my kids were calling, "You want to play ball? You want to play ball?" And I had to be careful not to say, "No-o-o, No-o-o. I am doing God's work right now. And boy, is it fun!"

Nearly every pastor needs to work more consistently and realistically on how important his or her family really is. The time investment has a payoff—it makes the children want to be near us, gives us a sense of family, and gives church members a model for how Christianity impacts the family.

Rest in your calling. The awareness of the calling has become very important to me at this time in my ministry. I do not have a career—I have a calling. God put me into the ministry. When you feel ready to quit, revisit God's call. You can rest in His call.

I remember a time when three guys chewed on me. They hit me for many things, ranging from music style to a kid wearing a baseball cap inside the church. All of a sudden, my mind tuned out and I saw myself sitting on a grass mower at a golf course. And I said to myself, "You can sit there for the rest of your life. You can just mow those little crisscross patterns on those greens. You can look back and say, "Man, that looks great. That really looks good.' Then you'd come back the next day and cut the greens another way."

All people have moments when they would like to quit, but you must remember your calling. If God called you to your present post of service, He will equip you and be with you. Rest in that calling, and it will keep you strong, courageous, and interested.

Refuse to let anything discourage you. You can get frustrated, but you must refuse ahead of time to let anything discourage you. Tell yourself, "It is just not going to happen. I am going to stay positive about this thing. I am walking with the Lord here."

When you are tempted to get discouraged, dump it on God. He is big enough to take it. When I whine, "God, I don't know about this," He answers with these thoughts: "Tell me where I hide the thunder. Tell me where the lightning is stored. Tell me where the hail is bound up" (see Job 38). I seem to hear the whole speech He gave Job. And He says, "It's going to be OK. I am in control. Come on, don't get discouraged. You hang in there."

Someone sent me these lines from Brennon Manning, and they sit on the back of my desk:

May all your expectations be frustrated.
May all your plans be thwarted.
May all your desires be withered into nothingness
that you may experience the powerlessness
and the poverty of a child.
And then sing and dance in the compassion of God
Who is Father, Son, and Holy Spirit.

The answer to most frustrations in ministry is right there—dependence on God.

CLARIFYING PRINCIPLES FROM JESUS

Here are several clarifying principles from Jesus that helped me lead my congregation through the transition of following a much-loved predecessor.

● *I must know who I am.* Jesus clearly understood himself when He said, "I am the light of the world . . . the Son of Man . . . the way and the truth and the life . . . the bread of life (John 8:12, Mark 14:62, John 14:6, John 6:35).

Don't compare yourself to someone else; just be who God wired you to be. God does not make clones. No two snowflakes and no two preachers are alike.

Take strength from scripture: "God gives us many kinds of

special abilities. . . . [and there] are different kinds of service to God. . . . There are many ways in which God works in our lives, but it is the same God who does the work in and through all of us who are his" (1 Cor. 12:4-6, TLB). God takes great delight in watching you be you!

• *I must know why I do what I do.* Jesus said, "I seek not to please myself but him who sent me" (John 5:30). Paul said, "We are not trying to please men but God, who tests our heart" (1 Thess. 2:4). Just play your life to an audience of One—the Sovereign God who set you apart for ministry.

A prayer that I read almost every week before I preach helps me keep focused on the One I am trying to please:

> O God, don't let the pulpit call me to the sermon . . . let the sermon call me to the pulpit. Before I break the bread of life, Lord, break me! Wash from my heart and lip the iniquity there . . . I want to preach, yeah, hemorrhage under the divine anointing. God, strip me of all pride . . . all cleverness . . . all showmanship . . . and personality . . . notes . . . canned quips and celestial clichés.
>
> Let me speak with the humility of Moses, the patience of Job, the wisdom of Paul, the power of Peter, and the authority of Christ.
>
> Lord, make my preaching clear, not clever; passionate, not pitiful; urgent, not "usual"; meaty, not murky. May it comfort the disturbed, disturb the comfortable, warn the sinner, mature the saint, give hope to the discouraged, and ready for heaven the whole audience.
>
> Let self be abased, Christ exalted, the Cross be central, and the plea be with passion. May my eyes never be dry. Just now, Lord, take me out of myself, usurp anything I've planned to say when it's in the way of YOUR message. Here I am, Lord. I'm your vessel. Amen (Source unknown).

Someone asked me what is different about my preaching now as compared to when I first started. I replied, "I really believe it now." Like Jeremiah said, it is a fire in your bones.

• *I must know what I want to accomplish.* Jesus said, "I must proclaim the good news . . . for I was sent for this purpose" (Luke 4:43, NRSV). Much of the time, what makes a pastor tired and gets him or her out of focus is that he or she is not really sure what to accomplish. Seek the face of God until you know what He wants you to accomplish in your present assignment.

Focus is pivotal but lacking in many ministries. If you are a golfer, a free-throw shooter, or a baseball player, you have to be focused. So what is my focus? I focus on my relationship with God, my relationship with my family, and my calling to preach the Good News.

● *I must share the load.* Jesus appointed 12 apostles, so He was years ahead of the management principle that it is better to get 10 people to work than to do the work of 10 people. It took me years to realize there is a synergistic dynamic that 10 people working together can accomplish significantly more than 10 times the work of one person.

> *God's great holy joke is this:*
> *Everyone that has ever walked this*
> *earth has had a messiah complex*
> *except for one, and He really was!"*
> —John Ortberg

In my work for Christ, I used to spin plates pretty well, something like the guy in the circus. That was my life, and that is what I did all day. But the Bible records 58 "one another" phrases. Still many pastors say, "I will do all the ministry." They seem to wear a big S (for super pastor) on their chest and fail to realize others have ministry gifts they need to use. Some pastors say by their actions, "I think of myself as a super pastor." In the process, they rob people of the blessing of using gifts God has given them.

John Ortberg wrote a great article about the messiah complex in *Leadership Journal.* He believes the main cause of ministerial fatigue is that many pastors have a messiah complex—we think we have to do it all. But when we reflect seriously about our work of ministry, we know our schedules are full. We know we feel forced to reject new ideas because we have no energy to invest in them. We realize that our standards of excellence are undermined because our involvement is spread too thin. And we know that our messiah complex keeps many gifted people from using their abilities for Kingdom causes.

The last paragraph of Ortberg's article was so insightfully convicting when he observed, "God's great holy joke is this: Everyone that has ever walked this earth has had a messiah complex except for one, and He really was!"

• *I must get alone with God.* That was the example of Jesus: "Crowds of people came to hear him and to be healed. . . . But Jesus often withdrew to lonely places and prayed" (Luke 5:15-16). Time alone with God determines how effective you will be when you are with people. I so often used to be like my Kodak vacation shots—overexposed and underdeveloped. Now I realize I must get alone with God often. I have found time with God to be the bottom-line secret of effective, satisfying ministry.

• *I must enjoy life.* In the midst of all the pressure of leading a church, you must take time to enjoy life. Practice some creative loafing. Wasn't it Shakespeare who said that it is better to have loafed and lost than never to have loafed at all? I think he might have said that. Build time in your date book for creative loafing and to enjoy life.

• *I must never stop learning.* One of the impressive things about the golfer Tiger Woods is the guy goes out and shoots a 66 and then goes to the practice tee. He keeps asking, "What am I doing wrong?" In ministry, I want to learn more. I want to be stretched to be a better leader. God needs pastors to do that, and our congregations need it too.

THE BOTTOM LINE OF EFFECTIVE TRANSITIONS

The summation of leading transitions in any church, in any setting, in any age, by any church leader, can be found in one sentence written by pastor Leith Anderson in *Leadership That Works:* "Leadership is figuring out what needs to be done and then doing it."

Vision and commitment are the two indispensable characteristics. That means taking risks for great causes, as Moses, Joshua, Peter, Stephen, and Paul did. They took risks as God opened their eyes to opportunities and possibilities. They could see more and farther than their contemporaries—and so can we, with God's help.

·6·

HOW WE KEPT (MOST) PEOPLE SMILING THROUGH TRANSITION

Mike Breaux

By perseverance the snail reached the ark.
—Charles Spurgeon

Transitions and changes happen to every church—all the time, everywhere—and with accelerating speed. Change flirts with us and frightens us. Transition sometimes comforts and often disturbs. Change requires risks but promises achievements. Some transitions are kind and loving; others are unbearable and miserable. But change is here to stay, so we must learn to use it for the Kingdom advantage.

Pastors usually champion changes they initiate and drag their feet concerning changes others propose. But change is a reality in culture and church. Paraphrasing Warren Bennis's concepts in *An Invented Life* as applied to the church, the pastors of effective churches for tomorrow will be maestros, not masters, and coaches, not commanders.

Even the most flexible people usually resist change that is forced upon them. Think about replacing your favorite suit or car—a great idea if you thought of it, but it seems incredibly unreasonable if someone else suggested it. Change is funny and confusing—it can be attractive, addictive, frightening, stimulating, or destructive.

But no one escapes change in our times. Like birth, taxes, and death—change is a part of life. Technology keeps creating more change in a year than our grandparents experienced in a lifetime. The church does not provide a safe place to hide from change and transition.

BREAKOUT PROGRESS OR STODGY COMFORT ZONES

In Kingdom issues, I am not interested in changing the changeless, but neither do I want to be like Martin Van Buren's mistaken position on transportation. In 1829, he wrote the following protest letter to the president of the United States: "The canal system of this country is being threatened by a new form of transportation known as railroads. As you may well know, railroad carriages are pulled at the enormous speed of 15 miles per hour by engines, endangering the life and limb of passengers. The Almighty never intended that people should travel at such break-neck speed!"

However, since radical change is a factor of contemporary life, it should not surprise pastors and church staff personnel that church members sometimes act as if they want their church to be a fortress where they can retreat from the chaos of our changing world. Though such security may seem attractive, no safe haven exists anywhere these days. Change-agent pastors do themselves and congregants a favor when they understand resistance to change may be rooted in fear, a reaction to an overdose of change in society, or a nostalgic memory of how predictable things used to be.

Then, too, the progress issue must be faced. In our heart of hearts, we know all progress requires someone to change. To this realization must be added the fact that a stubborn status quo can be more costly to a church than well-constructed change. But a much brighter possibility exists. So much has been written about resistance to change that it may be easy to forget that the church and its leaders can respond favorably to change. That is exactly the way a very large percentage of the people in our congregations have reacted. Transitions and newness are seen as a huge plus factor by many church members.

CHANGE AT HOME TOO

I have three kids, and that means constant changes in the family. When my oldest daughter, Jodi, was getting ready to go to Haiti as a missionary intern for a year, I was excited and scared. Her going meant change for our family that terrified me almost as much as my fear for her physical safety. When my son Derrick turned 16, he started driving. That was frightening from a safety perspective, but his driving represented a new independence for him and the reality that he was growing up, soon to be his own man. That meant serious change for our family, and while I welcomed the growth for him, I wished I could ignore many changes his growth brought him and us. My youngest son, Drew, while in his early teens was addicted to basketball, but I knew that his age meant great changes were around the corner for him and for our family. As you can see, I love change so long as it doesn't change my family too much. Often people at church are like me in my family. They know changes are inevitable, but that doesn't make them easy to accept.

> *Are we going to get fired up at halftime to play the rest of the game, or are we going to fold up and coast to the end?*

All these changes in the family made me think, "It's about half over for me." The sand seemed to be running at racetrack speed through the hourglass, and my hair went from fuzz to "wuzz"! These feelings, many of them frightening, encouraged me to read Bob Buford's book *Halftime or Game Plan?* I received insight when instead of calling these years a mid-life crisis, he calls it a halftime. Being involved in athletics all my life, I can relate to halftime. That means we have the third and fourth quarter to plan and make good.

The question is this—Are we going to get fired up at halftime to play the rest of the game, or are we going to fold up and coast to the end?

Buford's book provides a list of people and asks the reader to use one word to describe the meaning of each person's life. He gives examples like Mother Teresa—compassion, Christopher

Reeve—courage, Michael Jordan—competitiveness. Then he asks the reader to write his or her own name and add a word to describe himself or herself.

The word I chose was "change." The first half of my life has been about change. I have moved often. I have seen society change. I have seen my life change. I have served transitioning churches. I have served a brand-new church, a traditional church, and a contemporary church. These past several years have brought significant change—in my life, in my family, and in the churches I have served. I am a change agent. That's what God has called me to be even though I sometimes wish for more calm and less resistance.

Then Buford's book asks, What do you want the second half of your life to be? I did not list change, because I wanted the second half to be smooth sailing. But that's not likely to be true for anyone's ministry in these times, especially mine.

QUICK CHANGE AT CHURCH

When Southland Church was started in 1956 by Broadway Christian Church in Lexington, Kentucky, Wayne Smith was called to be the founding pastor. The church experienced amazing achievements through its 40-year history under his pastoral leadership. When I arrived, the church was strong—a congregation of loving people, an attitude they learned from their founding pastor. To this day, the congregation is loving, generous, and gracious—a special church any way you view it.

At the same time, however, they were tightly stuck in a traditional mode. It was the same people saying and doing the same thing—even singing the same songs. Everything was well done, but to attend church felt a lot like stepping back a few decades.

A few years ago while on vacation, I remember going to Southland Church wearing a golf shirt, jeans, and tennis shoes. At that time I thought, "I am the only one dressed like this. I feel out of it." Imagine what ideas bombarded my mind when they invited me to come as pastor. I felt, "Me? Me? I'm not sure that I belong here." But as God directed, I accepted the pastorate.

It soon became evident that to attract contemporary people, the church had to change—and change a lot. Maybe that is one reason they called me. Lay leaders felt the need. I felt the need.

Even Wayne Smith, the long-term founding pastor, told us changes were necessary. The staff suggested changes. All these changes were suggested so we could become more relevant to our culture and reach a new generation. So we made changes quickly. We moved fast, probably too fast.

My first Sunday, the screen came down from the ceiling and words went up. The hymnals were not used. A band and drama were added. The order of the service was extremely different. Many responded favorably the first week. "This was so refreshing! This was great!"

The next week, we did it again. They said, "This was good. Yeah, it was good." But you could sense some were not too sure.

The third week, some said, "Are we doing this every week?" It was as if they were thinking, "I guess the new guy's here, and he wants us to change!"

The purpose of change that I communicate in some way every Sunday is to do relevant things to reach people who do not know Christ. Southland Church is much different today than it was when I arrived. Though it is still a loving church, it is now clearly focused on winning lost people.

The contrast of starting a church for contemporary people in Las Vegas to leading a 40-year-old church through change in Kentucky has given me some ideas that I believe are worth sharing. Some I learned the hard way.

COMMITTING TO THE CHANGELESS GOSPEL WHILE MAKING THE CHURCH RELEVANT

In your own mind, think through the impact of changes, and be sure to bring lay leaders along in the process. Your commitment must be to help people know the difference between the abiding dimensions of the gospel and the changing strategies of communicating the gospel.

Jesus Christ is always the same. Heb. 13:8 reminds us that He is "the same yesterday and today and forever." What a magnificent source of strength that knowledge is to all believers.

The Word of God is changeless too. It has endured with surprising clarity across nearly 2000 years. Luke 21:33 tells us plainly that "heaven and earth will pass away, but my words will never pass away."

The gospel is changeless. Gal. 1:8-9 says that "even if we or an angel from heaven should preach a gospel other than the one we preached to you, let him be eternally condemned." We have a mandate to preach the unadulterated message of the shed blood of Christ on a cross—whether people like it or not.

In a society that embraces shifting worldviews, political correctness, and what I call talk-show truth, it is good to know that the gospel of Jesus Christ and the Cross never changes. And the church must never tamper with the changeless message.

SOME THINGS ALWAYS CHANGE

Some wise sage said, "Methods are many, principles are few. Principles never change, methods always do." Our task is to know the difference. Principles never change, but the ways we think about principles change, as do ways of behaving. Methods keep changing, so there are new ways to reach people with the old story.

Consider these changes: Paul wrote his messages with a quill and papyrus; I use a laptop. He shouted to be heard in the marketplace, and I use a lapel mike. He wore a toga, and our people are grateful I don't! My congregation drives to church in modern cars, while people from earlier times walked or rode horseback. The 90-year-old sage provided great insight when she said, "I want everything new and modern except my changeless faith."

*eaders with a brittle attitude
cause problems that set a church
back for years.*

Scripture teaches that the changeless God values freshness and newness. It is evident as one reads Scripture how many new things God wants to do. The Pharisees put God in a box when they insisted, "This is the way God is. He never changes."

On the contrary, God says, "I pour out new wine every day. I give you a new song to sing. I will give new mercies every day. I am building a new heaven and a new earth. The old order of things will pass away; behold I'm making all things new."

In Matt. 9:17, Jesus told the Pharisees, "Neither do men pour new wine into old wineskins. If they do, the skins will burst, the wine will run out and the wineskins will be ruined. No, they pour new wine into new wineskins, and both are preserved." Jesus is really saying if you want to partner with God, you cannot be brittle and inflexible.

I believe that God says, "Let Me pour new wine into you, Mike. Come on. Don't get so rigid and inflexible." If a leader is rigid and unbending when God tries to pour new wine into him or her, the wineskins break and turn his or her church into a mess. Leaders with a brittle attitude cause problems that set a church back for years. And churches divide more over method than message.

Traditions are hard to understand, question, and/or change. When the gospel's eternal newness is considered, it is amazing how churches hang on to old methods and lifeless traditions, as if they were unchangeable doctrine. Sometimes it's laughable, and sometimes I think God weeps.

Not too long ago, I was in a traditional church where it was decided Communion servers would serve from the back. The table was covered with a white cloth, which reminded me of the Shroud of Turin. So we were going to move the table to the back.

In the process of planning, we asked some of the older members about the significance of the cloth. One old lady said, "Well, honey, back then before air conditioning, the flies used to get in the juice, so we just covered it all up." That is an example of how some traditions were started—the conditions changed, but the practice continued.

To sort through issues where a church is stuck in a useless tradition, it helps me to remember how the great reformer Martin Luther impacted his culture. He put holy words to an unforgettable tune that music historians say was taken from the tavern when he wrote "A Mighty Fortress Is Our God." We now say that's a hymn. It is amazing how we elevate common things to a sacred status when God wants to pour new wine into contemporary ministries. He wants us to use new strategies to reach people with the everlasting gospel.

STRATEGIES WE LEARNED FOR MAKING CHANGES

Keep sensitive to the Holy Spirit. At our church, we try to listen to God as we pray. Ideally, all change worth doing in any church would have the Lord's approval and be pleasing to Him. Like many other congregations, we have decision groups that sometimes have trouble agreeing on the color of the carpet or the brand of lawn mower to purchase. And our church has thoughtfully developed procedures and policies for nearly every eventuality.

Surprisingly, they put aside their carefully crafted procedures when they called me as senior pastor because of what they believed to be the leading of the Holy Spirit. He sometimes does that to our usual ways of doing church.

The challenge for all of us is to have enough humility to not get in front of Him and say, "My agenda!" and at the same time to have the courage not to lag behind Him. Sometimes God says, "Come on, get out of the boat!"

The challenge is to walk in step with the Spirit, which requires that a group of leaders must pray and listen to God. Isa. 30:21 helps me: "Whether you turn to the right or to the left, your ears will hear a voice behind you, saying, 'This is the way; walk in it.'" Where the Holy Spirit is welcomed and invited, He leads us. Lead us—that is what God wants to do with us.

Keep sensitive to people's needs. Change can be made as a reasonable process or with searing pain. Our leaders have discovered there is more than one way to face transitions.

A friend of mine made this observation about how we sometimes work at Southland Church: "Sometimes you make decisions like tearing adhesive tape off a man's chest. Then when people scream, you put your arms around them and say, 'It's going to be OK!'" And my friend was right. But we have learned tape comes off with much less pain if its soaked in soap and water. The lesson—the decision processes would take place with much less resistance if we developed a greater sensitivity to the people who will be affected by the process.

In light of these concerns, our leaders decided we would make change easier for people to understand by always stating a reason or reasons behind each decision. We are committed to loving people and realize that some changes have emotional content as well as eternal implications. We are going to be sensitive to people when changes have to be made. And we are determined to make changes that will meet the needs of the entire congregation rather than hold the whole body captive to the negative feelings of a few.

A lot of changes were implemented right after I became pastor. Lay leaders decided to kill the "come on back again" Sunday night service that had less than 50 attending.

They said, "We're going to bag it."

And I thought, "I know who'll get blamed for this one. It's going to be me."

The decision group said, "You would like to do a Wednesday night service, wouldn't you?"

I said, "Well, I would like to do one down the road."

So they said, "We'll kill the Sunday night service so you can start a service on Wednesday night."

So we switched. Now 2,000 people are on our campus Wednesday night to study, worship, and be with God. That was a courageous move on our leadership's part, but one they felt the Holy Spirit directed them to do.

I remember one elder saying, "You know what, nothing sweeps clean like a new broom!"

I said, "Yeah, but I'm the broom you guys are sweeping with." It was scary for me as the new pastor. But we have learned that changes are much more acceptable when leaders seek and follow the guidance of the Holy Spirit.

Tie change to core values. Listening led our church committees to develop core values. These values are used to shape the details of the church's ministry and have been communicated over and over to the entire congregation.

I talk about the values everywhere and all the time.

One core value for us is an "excellence that honors God and reflects His character," and I talk about that often. Some of our other core values are these:

- Lost people matter to God; therefore, they matter to us.
- Ministry is accomplished best in teams.
- Authenticity glorifies God and frees people.

• Worship is a lifestyle expressed with private consistency and corporate vibrancy.

We talk about these issues over and over. I slide them into all kinds of conversations so our people understand the core values that shape our ministry. As a result, our people realize we do not make changes just for change's sake.

Clarify the urgency behind the why. I think this is important to explain why the changes are being made. Remind the church that even though society is so messed up, we have the answer in Jesus Christ our Lord. What a time to be the Church! Christ compels us to win the many people out there who do not know Him, but we have to make some changes to reach them.

Get intentional about ministry in contemporary culture. A friend of mine, Dick Alexander, made this observation in his church newsletter:

It is interesting to read church papers. Often when a change is made in a church program, long apologetic explanations will be given. Isn't that backwards? Shouldn't it be that the churches that aren't regularly making changes in their programs have to explain why? It has been said, "If it ain't broke, don't fix it." But in church terms, any church in an urban area that is not steadily growing is already broken. Whether it's broken isn't a matter of whether we like it this way but whether it's changing people's lives.

One of the ways that we try to effect change is by stating, "We're just trying to get more intentional about presenting Christ in our culture."

There is an urgency about all of this. Two-and-a-half billion nonbelievers live within the shadows of church buildings around the world. We do need more missionary effort to reach the unreached people of the world. Half the world's population can be reached by existing churches if they'll just do it. How many non-Christians complain, though, that they are not interested in church because it changes too fast? Isn't it that usually church is too dull? Churches are very concerned about losing members if their people don't like changes. Are they at least as concerned for the 2.5 billion that are already lost?

Resist the labels and go for relevant. In the past 4½ years at Southland, 3,200 people have made a decision for Christ—over half are first-time commitments. It has just been awesome. I attribute those responses to our church leaders being courageous enough to say, "We are going to reach the unreached people of this area! No more playing church!"

One of the ways that we try to effect change is by stating, "We're just trying to get more *intentional* about presenting Christ in our culture." This key purpose statement continually ties us to our mission. Our mission statement says we want to connect the unconnected into a relationship with Jesus Christ and then together grow in full devotion to Him. This is a two-pronged statement built on the Great Commission of reaching the lost and then discipling them in the ways of Christ. That is our intention, and we seek to make our purpose plain all the time. That is what we are about. That is our business. We want to be intentional about doing our main business.

In talking to our church body, we try not to use the labels "contemporary" and "traditional." Sometimes people try to trap me into using those terms, but I reply, "No, we're going to be relevant." Our heartbeat is to reach lost people. That's what drives us. And we are always trying to figure out how we can best do that.

Know the land mines, and choose your battles. There are some land mines you do not want to mess with when you are trying to make changes. Figure out what or who they are. Talk to people about them, and if they say don't go there, then don't go there.

God will bring changes in His timing. Some things are not worth going to the mat for. Some things are. Others do not really matter.

Even though you may be strongly opinionated about a given issue, just let it slide. God will bring it up in His timing. Then

He will give you the courage to do it. You are going to make a lot of enemies in the process, and then when it is all said and done, you will go, "Well, so what! Why was I so fired up about that? That wasn't as big a deal as I thought it was."

Love people through changes. Make friends with those who oppose you. Make friends of critics. I learned that during church the people who have the greatest struggle are not bad people at all. Usually they are the people who have been there the longest, and they are the ones who go through the most grief. They may feel that their memories get trampled. Those are the people you have to love and help through the changes.

The three-steps-forward-two-steps-backward formula. Three steps forward and two steps back equals one step ahead. Sometimes you have to push the envelope three steps forward. Then someone says, "I don't know about that!" So you back up two steps, but you are at least one step ahead of where you were. Sometimes you just move ahead as you ask yourself, "How far can I go until somebody pulls me back?" Then you pull back two steps.

Admit your failure. When you make a change that falls flat, admit it. Laugh at yourself. Say, "We shouldn't have done it. That was dumb. We did it too fast and stepped out ahead of the Holy Spirit."

Take the blame: "When it was all said and done, it was my ego that got in the way. It was my agenda. It wasn't God's." That makes you more authentic, a lot more transparent. So admit your mistakes. Refuse to spend energy and goodwill on some decision that is not working. Back up and start again.

Applaud life transformations. Share how changes are producing the desired results of your core values in real people. We have testimonies from people about what God is doing in their lives. These reports of transformed lives energize a church.

I met a new convert the other day who said he was "into drugs and alcohol and everything else you can imagine! I was as far away from God as probably anybody you ever met!"

I said, "No, I worked in Vegas . . ."

He said, "I don't care—I was farther; I don't want to get into it with you; trust me, I was farther!"

Then he said, "Even my wife told me, 'You know what you

need to do? You need to give God a shot! I challenge you to give Him 30 days, and if He doesn't prove himself in 30 days, then I won't bug you about this God stuff again.' I said, 'OK, deal.'"

He was sitting in my office, and he started crying as he said, "Man, she brought me here. It took about 10 days!" He said, "I just fell apart! I knew I needed God in my life. I have been a Christian now for about six months. I wanted to introduce myself to you and let you know that I have been sitting out there in the church listening every Sunday. My life is changed."

He continued, "I feel like God is leading me to be a minister. How do you do that?"

This guy wanted to make his life work. I said to him, "You are a poster child for our church! We are trying to take this raw material of someone who is so far away from God and turn that person into a fully devoted follower of Christ. You are what we are trying to do!"

Big hairy audacious goals. I realize the title seems a bit out of place in church, so let's settle for BHAG (pronounced BEE-hag). It means this goal is so big, I am going to have to change some things to reach it. For example, I heard Jim Collins say, "I'm going to read 100 books in a year." So he bought some furniture and reading lamps, sat down in his chair, got *War and Peace* in one hand and Monday night football on TV. Soon he said, "Nothing is happening." After about an hour and a half of watching Monday night football and not turning one page in this book, he called his brother-in-law and said, "Come and get my TV and never bring it back. If you bring it back, I will shoot you!" He said he got rid of the TV and read 100 books that year. That was his BHAG. What BHAG do you want to accomplish? And if you want to accomplish it, what has to be unplugged in your life?

So as a church, set some BHAGs. Then to get there, realize some things have to be unplugged along the way. Only you can determine your BHAGs and then decide what has to be changed in your church to accomplish them.

At Southland Church, we have some BHAGs. In the next five years, we hope to be a church of 10,000 people. To do that, we are going to have to build a new facility because we are "maxed out."

We want to have 500 small groups functioning in five years. That means 5,000 adults in small groups. That's a BHAG for us. To get there, we have to make some changes. But the possibility of accomplishing those two BHAGs are worth almost any change. We will change, and God will honor us with new people.

BEARING THE PAIN AND ENJOYING THE GAIN

All pastors grieve when even one person disagrees with them and leaves the church. It really hurts when the reason appears to be some change you championed. The dilemma is almost impossible to avoid. Progress means change, and change at church threatens some people.

Die to your desires that everyone will love you and accept your ideas.

Throughout this chapter, I have emphasized over and over that change in the church must be subjected to the guidance of the Lord. Change must never be made for the sake of change, but always for the purpose of reaching more and more lost people. Often because they pushed for change among religious people, Moses, David, Paul, and Jesus had their critics and detractors. And you will have yours too.

The change-agent pastoral leader must always check his or her motives. The right reason must be driving the change. When motives are right, it is easier to accept the negative, reactionary individual, to examine key strategies, to express love to critics, and to change for the greatest good for the most people. Do your best. Check your insecurity at God's door, and die to your desires that everyone will love you and accept your ideas. Count on being challenged and sometimes misunderstood. Then lead from a moral center with a holy passion for winning and for discipling as many as you can for the glory of God. You and your church will survive and even thrive by effectively implementing the Great Commission where you are.

7

A CENTER CITY CHURCH EXPERIENCES NEW BIRTH

William Hinson

Christians are supposed not merely to endure change,
nor even to profit by it, but to cause it.
—H. M. Fosdick

OLD FIRST CHURCH DOWNTOWN

Old "First" churches in the downtowns of America have been on the endangered species list for many years. Since 1900, approximately 40,000 such churches have closed. Population shifts have occurred, and people have migrated to the suburbs. In addition, urban blight has struck in many places, lending to the perception that downtown is unattractive as well as unsafe.

When I arrived in Houston in June of 1983, the church to which I had been assigned was an example of the general trend across America. First United Methodist Church Houston was a great preaching place with a crowded sanctuary each Sunday morning. Throughout the mid-'80s, I preached to large crowds that spilled over into every nook and cranny of our building. Our sanctuary was so crowded that people sat on the stairs on all special days and at least seven other Sundays during the year. Such crowds can be very seductive and conducive to a general feeling of complacency concerning the spiritual health and vitality of a congregation.

A closer examination of the church to which I had been appointed revealed that our Sunday School attendance had been in decline for a number of years and our stewardship level was extremely low. Although we had a lot of money in the bank, almost $300,000, we found it extremely difficult, if not impossible, to support our staff, pay our apportionments, develop a program, and keep up our building. We also had a huge amount of deferred maintenance.

Just prior to my arrival, the church had sold the last foot of property it owned in downtown Houston and placed the money into a newly established foundation. The only land the church possessed after that sale was the downtown church site. This action had, consciously or unconsciously, produced a kind of siege mentality. A well-known, popular pastor was retiring after 23 years, and many assumed the church would settle down and reflect on the glory days of her past. That mentality was having a deadly effect upon our congregation.

THE LATE '80s: WHEN FIRST CHURCH JOINED THE TREND IN AMERICAN PROTESTANTISM

The radiant center that was downtown Houston began to deteriorate in the late '80s. Retail merchants began to leave en masse, and the homeless problem hit our community in earnest. The view of downtown began to change, and it had nothing to do with the facts. A survey printed in the local papers revealed that better than 50 percent of the people of Houston openly declared that they would not go downtown for any reason. The perception was that it was unsightly, full of empty buildings, and unsafe. In reality, serious crime in downtown Houston was lower than the crime rate in the suburbs. We discovered, however, that perception is reality.

Simultaneously with the retail shift out of downtown Houston, there was a move on the part of major television networks to exclude organized religion. A number of ministerial scandals had shaken our nation, and apparently the networks concluded it was a good time to shift religious programming. Unfortunately, there was no substantial outcry from the community. The church had televised its services since the mid-'50s. We had enjoyed live telecasts, free of charge, from 11 A.M. to 12 noon each Sunday. This change, combined with the change in downtown Houston, had a devastating effect on our membership. The yearly first-time visitors' list was reduced from approximately 3,000 to

1,000. The decline occurred within two years. The number of our new members, a 624 annual average for the previous seven years, began to decline. We shifted our television ministry to independent stations, but we lacked the kind of coverage we had previously enjoyed. Staying even in our membership now began to be a battle.

Max Dupree has said that our first task is to define reality.

There were other indications that we were lacking vitality at First Church. Financial problems continued. We were still taking in new members, but we were pressed to identify any real areas of growth. Attendance was static. The youth group and the children's department were extremely small. The time had come for a careful study of where we were and where God wanted us to go.

A SELF-STUDY: OUR FIRST SNIFF OF REALITY

Max Dupree has said that our first task is to define reality. Nothing can be done until this is accomplished. But our experience was that this first task was, perhaps, our most difficult task. We had lived with our perceptions so long that we found it difficult to set them aside and come to terms with reality.

Our Trustees appointed a Long-Range Planning Committee in late 1989. The committee was composed of some of our finest leaders and visionaries. They were to be amenable to the Board of Trustees.

After some months of self-study, it became obvious that we were having difficulty being objective. We sought and found outside help in the person of Carl George. Mr. George at first refused to take us on as a client because of his overcrowded schedule. When he realized, however, that First Church Houston desired to make changes, he said, "I cannot refuse any United Methodist church that is serious about change. Most Methodist churches," he said, "choose to die with dignity. If you are serious about change, I will rearrange my schedule and be your consultant." We assured him that we were serious, and he joined us in our all-important task of defining reality.

One of Carl George's first steps was an extensive survey of our congregation. He discovered that our people were extremely happy with their church. They even liked their preacher. They liked things just the way they were, and almost no one was interested in any change. Those studies revealed that between 2 and 3 percent of our children had been lost each year for the past 30 years. The same was true of our youth. A demographic study of our congregation showed our people to be middle to upper class economically, but our giving still had not progressed to the point of giving us financial relief. When I arrived in 1983, the average pledge had been between $600 and $700 per year. That number had increased only minimally by 1989 when Mr. George began his survey. We were operating under the enormous assumption that "First Church doesn't have any financial problems, and we are 'a rich church.'" In the meantime, we were experiencing mold load from our central plant that was in desperate need of replacement. Our trips to the throat specialists were an eloquent testimony to the internal problems of our building.

We had replaced the broken windows in our building but were still plagued with a deteriorating roof. Our deferred maintenance bill continued to increase.

Perhaps the most troubling finding in our self-study was the average age of our congregation. That average age was in excess of 60 and increasing rapidly. We had comforted ourselves that even during the hard times of the late '80s we were still "holding our own." In reality, we were declining. No church "holds its own"; it is either getting older and smaller or younger and larger. First Church was getting older.

Each day's mail brought another heartbreaking letter to this pastor. They were all basically the same. "We love First Church. We met here and were married in this beautiful sanctuary. Now that our children have come, however, and are interested in scouting, in recreation, and in other activities, we find it necessary to attend a neighborhood church where the facilities and programs are readily available. Please remember that we love you and we will pray for you." We had long suspected, because of the steady flow of letters like that one, that we had lost an entire generation at First Church. We had more empty nesters than any other church, but in that all-important bracket of 30 to 50, we were very slim.

Our outside consultant forced us to be objective. We looked at the erosion of denominational loyalty, the insistence of a full-orbed program for children and youth, and the nature of our competition from other churches providing the programs we could not provide in downtown Houston. We began to see that if we were to survive as a major force in Houston, dramatic changes would have to occur.

"IT WILL KILL US TO CHANGE; WE HAVE TO CHANGE"

In the process of examining ourselves, the long-range Planning Team also sought a vision for what First Church should be. With each passing week, it became more obvious that the dreams we had for our church, such as a great program of recreation and a Christian school, could not be fulfilled on a half block of land in downtown Houston. Such realizations led one member of our group to declare, "It will kill me to change, but we have to change if we are to survive."

Our thorough demographic study gave us a clear idea of where our members lived. The vast majority of our people lived to the west and southwest of downtown. Another study revealed that in the decade between 1980 and 1990, the population within 5 miles of downtown had declined, while the population within 10 miles had increased slightly, and the population just outside of 10 miles had increased dramatically. The geographical center of our membership, it was determined, was 6 miles west and south of downtown—just south of the Galleria area on Loop 610. Of the people who were visiting, 82 percent of them came from the west and southwest of downtown.

These discoveries led us to establish a site selection team to begin looking at the feasibility of a relocation of our church. Such study involved, of course, connectional considerations, how we could relocate our large congregation without being intrusive on other congregations, and other considerations.

After extensive study, we began to zero in on the exact geographical center of our membership, namely the Galleria area.

The Trustees and Long-Range Planning Team recommended that we relocate to this area. Before we could carry that recommendation to the congregation, however, we had to do our relocation due diligence.

Closer study revealed that our athletic fields posed zoning difficulties and that there was strong resistance from other United Methodist congregations in the area. The District Board of Church Locations was reluctant to give us approval to move, and one of the bishops opposed the location. All of these factors combined to stymie any idea of a congregational vote to purchase the property near the Galleria.

GO WEST, OLD CHURCH, GO WEST

While we were experiencing considerable problems with our connectional considerations, we were also looking more closely at the implications of leaving the neighborhood where our church had served since 1839. We were the last of the large Protestant churches remaining downtown. City officials came and begged us to stay because we were a landmark for Houston. Since morale was as low as it was at that time, they felt our departure would send a signal to the entire Houston area that would have dreadful implications for downtown. Besides these considerations, we had, through a vigorous Missions Work Area, developed any number of ministries in downtown Houston that would, of necessity, be abandoned if we should leave our downtown location.

The same demographic study that showed that the preponderance of our members lived in West Houston also revealed that there were approximately 3,000 members who lived east and north of the city. What would be their response to driving six miles more to get to church? There were also historical considerations.

Most of the pastors in the Texas Conference had been ordained at the altar of our church. The first Conference Between Christians and Jews was held in our building. Many other important events had transpired there. We began to come to terms with our hidden legacy and all of the implications stemming from our long heritage in downtown Houston.

The Long-Range Planning Team and the Trustees found

themselves in a deep tension between our need to stay downtown and a definite need to migrate to the growth corridor of our city to the west. The Site Selection Team had searched throughout the 610 area and had decided upon the Galleria site as the best for our relocation. Other church members had unofficially begun their search. A site discovered by one of our Trustees was the Beltway 8-Westpark site involving 27.3 acres. Investigation revealed that this property was available for $7 million but had an appraised value in excess of $8 million.

All of these factors combined to lead us to a dual campus. We had not consciously decided for this option. The decision evolved over a period of time as a part of an unfolding planning process and, we believe, the guidance of Almighty God. Our Trustees and our Long-Range Planning Team came to the realization at about the same time that we did not have to make an either/or decision. We could say yes to those members who wanted us to stay in downtown Houston and yes to those who wanted us to expand our ministry base to the growth corridor of our city. We could have a dual campus.

A COSTLY LEAK

First Church Houston was built on some land given to our members by the Allen brothers, the founders of Houston. The church is nearly as old as the city and is a high-visibility church. News reporters love to get a scoop about First Church. The reason for this is twofold: the church has a long history in downtown, and it has been the leading television congregation in the city since the mid-'50s.

Many of our members are empty nesters. Some left First Church when their children were small but returned when their children had grown and moved away. Many were tired of the hustle and bustle of the suburban church with all of its accompanying demands relative to children and youth. They returned to First Church for "good music and good preaching." The last thing they wanted from First Church was to be confronted with the kind of radical plan about to be presented by the Long-Range Planning Team and the Trustees.

Somehow—no one knows how—a reporter learned about our dual-campus proposal and wrote a story. The first word our people had about a shift in focus was through the local newspaper. To say that some PR problems were created by this development is a huge understatement!

The oil company from whom we were buying the 27 acres began to realize that property values were rapidly increasing in that section of Houston, destined to be the population center by the year 2004. They issued a purchase deadline. If the church did not purchase the property by December 1, 1992, they were going to take it off the market. We had a major job to achieve with our congregation and a short time in which to do it.

WE NEEDED MORE THAN FACTS

he good news is, when you turn the head of the horse, sooner or later the rest of the body will follow."
—Generation to Generation

In the midst of our communication blitz—our home meetings, our congregational meetings, and others—in which we were presenting the facts of a dual-campus church, it became obvious that we had a strong minority who had determined not to go that way. I vividly recall a lunch with my predecessor. Dr. Allen, who was supportive of me, tried to persuade me to drop the whole proposal. He promised that pursuing the dual campus plan would be the most difficult thing I had ever attempted. I agreed. I knew that it was going to be tough. I asked him, however, how long he thought First Church could endure as a viable church if the present trend continued. He responded with unforgettable words, "God Almighty can't keep that congregation for 15 more years." Following his declaration, I knew that I had my answer. I could not simply go off into a comfortable retirement wondering whether or not we could have turned this church around if only I had been willing to run the risk of incurring the displeasure of a vocal minority.

A late-night call from Carl George reinforced my decision. Carl quoted a line from the book *Generation to Generation*. He told me, "The good news is, when you turn the head of the horse, sooner or later the rest of the body will follow." Then he added, "The bad news is, you are the head of the horse." He knew that the next few years were going to be very challenging.

I prepared a series of sermons, accompanying all the rest of our communication, titled "Our Church: A Monument or a Mission Station in the 21st Century?" Before that series was completed, it was apparent to the entire membership that their pastor of 10 years did not believe we had a viable future if the present trends continued and we did not make a dramatic move. People began to leave, many of whom I considered close friends. A member of the Committee on Finance was among them. He said, "We can't raise enough money to run one campus, let alone two." We proceeded, in the midst of a great deal of anguish, to develop a business plan for the implementation of a master plan that an architect had prepared for the development of our 27 acres. We showed the congregation our plan, told them of our proposal, and how we could pay for it. On July 19, 1992, we had our church conference. People voted 64 percent in favor, 32 percent opposed, 4 percent in abstention. We knew that with 32 percent in open disagreement after we had given it our best shot, we had a recipe for pain.

One of the interesting facts, however, about 1992, the year of our big decision, was that in spite of our membership loss, we set records in money given. In every presentation of our plan, we had shared a vision for a vital congregation in the growth corridor appealing primarily to families, serving the entire community, including a recreation program and a Christian school. We learned firsthand that money follows vision. People had never given big money for maintenance. It began to flow from unexpected places when the vision took root in the hearts of our visionary people.

Two Hundred Pioneers

Immediately following our historic vote, we invited pioneers to join us for the adventure of beginning a new congregation in West Houston. We began with home groups and occasional celebrations in which I would cast the vision. In the home groups, training was conducted for small-group leaders.

Our first service was held on the second Sunday of January 1993, in a neighborhood elementary school. Later we worshiped in the ballroom of a nearby hotel, and then in the spring of 1994 we found a home. Two and a half acres with two office buildings became available directly across the street from our 27 acres. We purchased the 2.5 acres and two buildings for a million dollars, with one of them on a long-term lease producing about $55,000 to $60,000 a year in revenue. We renovated one of the buildings, converting it into classrooms and an interim worship center.

Those in business smiled at God's provision and reminded the congregation that for a million-dollar investment we were getting 6 percent interest and a free home. The First United Methodist Church Westchase began to grow.

MEANWHILE, BACK AT THE RANCH

No one who saw the emptying of the downtown area in the late '80s could have imagined that we would see the greening of downtown in the mid-'90s. Developers began to build loft apartments in empty downtown buildings and also to build apartments in the midtown area. With the decision to build a new baseball stadium in downtown, restaurants and theaters began to appear; retailers began to return; and for the first time in 50 years, our downtown congregation began to receive members who walk to church. In recent months, 9,000 residents have been added to the downtown zip code.

One of the most gratifying things about our dual campus has been the experience of seeing our average age decrease. It is dramatically younger now—probably in the 40s. One unexpected development, however, is that even apart from the Westchase Campus, the Downtown Campus is growing younger. As a matter of fact, in 1999 the average age of new members joining Downtown was below that of the average age of those persons joining at the Westchase Campus. We are delightfully surprised to be experiencing increased vitality in every way on the Downtown Campus.

THE FABRIC WAS TORN

The power of the vision for the Westchase Campus was not lost on those who attend Downtown. They, together with our leadership team, began to dream new dreams for Downtown with this growing revitalization. As we began to capitalize on the new growth downtown, it became obvious that the inner system of our church had been somewhat strangled prior to the development of the Westchase Campus. We would not have taken advantage of the revitalization of the downtown area if we had not experienced the trauma of giving birth to a second congregation. Downtown was more open to new leadership and to change itself because of the new campus. That openness has begun to pay dividends.

THE EIGHT-STAGE PROCESS FOR CREATING CHANGE

Since going through our transition experiences, someone gave me a copy of John J. Kotter's "The Eight-Stage Process of Creating Major Change." I was pleased to see that we had done

Help everyone see the impending crisis or great opportunity before you.

most of the stages right. How helpful it would have been to have had this list earlier. To understand how to make the process orderly and to keep from being mesmerized by vocal opposers, I suggest every pastor view this list. It is an encouragement to know someone else has already faced what we face. Here is the list from Kotter's impressive book *Leading Change;* the comments are mine.

1. **Establish a sense of urgency.** Help everyone see the impending crisis or great opportunity before you. Sometimes a window of opportunity presents itself that was not there yesterday or will not be there tomorrow.

2. **Create a guiding coalition.** Put a team together, and give them power and authority to lead the needed change.

3. **Develop a vision and strategy.** Work with the coalition

team to move from concept to achievement. Use the vision as an evaluation standard for everything you do. Eliminate or refocus activities, expenditures, and programs that are not consistent with your vision.

4. **Communicate the change vision.** Use every communication channel you have to explain and inspire the needed change. Never underestimate how many church members have no idea of what is being done.

5. **Empower board-based action.** Identify the hindrances. Encourage risk taking and keep reminding the congregation that a change is for an important reason and never just for the sake of more change.

6. **Generate short-term wins.** Talk about the improvement resulting from the change. One pastor I know who was leading a congregation through a major building program reported achievement along the way by saying things like this: "This week the plans were finished and are they beautiful." "The loan was approved this week at a lower interest rate than we could have ever imagined." "This week the walls went up, and you can now see how spacious the new building is going to be."

7. **Consolidate gains and produce more changes.** The idea is to establish enough credibility in the first six steps so people will be willing to trust you with more authority and influence. Protect your credibility from being compromised. And when the confidence is given, make sure you are trustworthy and honest so they continue to believe in you.

8. **Anchor new approaches to the culture.** This principle means the church must make sense to those who attend and be relevant to those you want to win. The principle also allows for another truth: Transitions that have been forced on the church by changes in society are not all negative.

⁸

USING THE JESUS MODEL OF PERSISTENCE AND PATIENCE

Gene Appel

The wonder and curiosity which welcomes what is new and regards it not as threatening but enriching life— that wonder and curiosity is from God.
—Harry Williams

Every summer our family vacations on a Minnesota lake where my parents started going in the '40s. Our favorite fishing spot is about 20 miles from our cabin. To get there, we have to trailer our boat and launch on a busy lake. The first lake, where we launch the boat, has many cabins along its shoreline, dozens of other boats, and lots of water-skiers. But there is a natural channel in the middle of all that activity that most fishers and water-skiers never think to explore. The secret channel is about two football fields long and 6 feet wide, covered by lily pads and lined with a wall of white birch trees on each side. As you motor through this channel, you feel a bit like Ponce de León on an adventuresome discovery. The water gets so shallow you have to lift the boat's motor. The last 50 feet of the channel gets even more shallow so you have to wade beside the boat. But the effort is richly rewarded as the channel opens to an incredibly beautiful remote lake. There are only two cabins on the shores of this lake and only a few other boats. Deer come down to drink at the lake. Eagles fly overhead. And the fishing is beyond description.

he lake beyond the channel is
where the better fishing is.

I always ask myself this every summer: Since the second lake is so beautiful and such a great fishing spot, why do so few people go there? Why is the first lake so overpopulated with fishers and boats? Why aren't more of them on the quiet lake where the fishing is so much better? The answer is simple—it takes extra effort to get there. One has to imagine, prepare, and put forth extra energy to experience the better lake.

THE CHANNEL OF CHANGE ALWAYS REQUIRES EFFORT

Churches are often like folks on the first lake. They would rather not consider the channel of change.

Their reasons vary. Some say this is the church as it has always been, or this is the church as we like it. They reason, to get to something better, we would have to pass through this change channel, and that creates confusion and demands work. Getting through the channel can be difficult, so many church leaders never even try. But let's not forget—the lake beyond the channel is where the better fishing is.

Locating and going through such a change channel was where I found myself when I arrived at Central Christian Church in Las Vegas, Nevada. I accepted the leadership challenge of that church with the desire that it would become a relevant, contemporary, cutting-edge, seeker-targeted, highly evangelistic, discipling church—a radically different kind of church than it had always been. There was one slight problem—this was a very traditional-style church, and many of the people liked it the way it was.

It is hard to believe there is a traditional anything in glitzy Las Vegas, but Central Church was about as traditional as any church in the heartlands or on New England shores. Two factors had to be faced. Many, perhaps most, members liked the church the way it was. And attendance was in decline.

Let me describe the church I found. The choir was robed. The organ was used in every service. The doxology was always sung as the deacons brought the offering plates to the Communion table. The Lord's Prayer was recited in every Sunday morning service. Only a fraction of the people attended the only discipling ministry, a traditional Sunday School. Every decision required the approval of three boards—the Elder Board, the Deacon Board, and the Official Board. The results—decisions always took at least three months. Women were seen and not heard, though they might be allowed to sing a solo, join the choir, or teach a children's class. Spiritual gifts were rarely mentioned. Attendance had been in decline for five straight years. And the membership was mostly gray haired.

It was obvious that the church I dreamed of Central becoming would have to be led through a channel of change. And I was their leader.

You may wonder why I agreed to go to such a church. There were two important reasons.

One reason was a sense of calling that God wanted a church like my dream in Las Vegas, one of the most spiritually needy cities in the world. Las Vegas is also one of the fastest growing cities in the United States. And *Psychology Today* says it is the most stressful city in America, leading the nation in alcoholism, suicides, divorces, and incarcerations. I believed that a Jesus-built church that the gates of hell could not prevail against was needed in such a setting of population growth and spiritual poverty.

The second reason that captured my interest was that I sensed key lay leaders wanted to change the status quo, though they did not know what that might mean. Some of them believed something needed to change even though everything looked as if it was going reasonably well. Apparently they agreed with Danny Cox, who writes in *Leadership When the Heat's On:* "Continued belief in the sacredness of an organization's way of doing things will ultimately lead to disaster."

One clue that the leaders were willing to take a risk was that I was 25 years old when they called me and had never been a senior pastor. The church had been on a senior pastor search for more than a year and had introduced eight or nine candidates to the congregation. Eventually, the committee came to the congregation and said, "We want to call a 25-year-old minister who has never been a senior pastor. He has absolutely no experience, but we think this is God's guy for us."

As you might guess, that proposal was not well received by everyone in this aging congregation.

So when they called me, I said to myself, "This is an unusual group of leaders who might be willing to do just about anything." And they have proven that to be true over the years.

When I arrived at Las Vegas, we were a church of about 400 people. There were four other staff members, and I was by far the youngest. In those years, I was often asked what it was like to be senior pastor and at the same time the "baby" of the staff. To be candid, my youth usually worked to my advantage. When things went well, people said, "Wow, he's just a kid." And when I bombed, people were forgiving by saying, "Well, he's just a beginner."

I knew the journey through the channel of change would not be easy. I heard stories of churches trying to navigate major transitional, transformational changes, only to end up with cataclysmic explosions. I heard about congregations "growing" over night from 500 to 150. I heard about terrible church splits. And I heard about pastors being forced out of the ministry. I heard about ministers who quit out of frustration. I heard about broken relationships among people who had been friends for years. I thought there must be a better way.

Some churches might allow a leader to initiate major transformational change immediately, but they are rare exceptions. Central Church was not one of them, and I knew it. Sometimes churches are ready to do anything to get past a major crisis, such as a fire or the death of a beloved leader. Sometimes a church is so dead that transformational change is the only way the congregation can survive. That was not our situation. There was no frightening crisis. There had been no warring factions or mass exodus. Most members felt the church was healthy even though it had not been growing. So it seemed to me that if transformational change was to take place, it would have to be at a methodical pace or the whole situation could just blow up.

TOUGH QUESTION CREATED TURNING POINT

The turning point for moving out of the past came when we were willing to ask ourselves a painful question that turned out to be the defining issue for our church. I had been there a couple of years when we asked and tried to answer this question: How do we measure up to the biblical purpose of what a church is supposed to be?

Now, it would have been easier not to ask that question. Things were going well. During my first couple of years at Central we reestablished church health. We reversed the downward trend. From all measurements typically used to evaluate a church, we looked successful. Attendance was up, the staff was being enlarged, and we were in an expansion building program. Finances were good; the spirit was positive. It would have been easy to deceive ourselves into thinking all was well in our corner of Christendom.

We were not experiencing Kingdom expansion but Kingdom redistribution.

But then we asked a nagging question, and the church was forced by the obvious answer to change.

KINGDOM REDISTRIBUTION FRIGHTENED US

When we measured ourselves against what we understood the biblical purpose of the church to be, the kingdom of God was not expanding much. As we considered the biblical standard, we discovered that increased attendance was 75 percent transfer growth—people who were already believers in Christ. Only 25 percent was conversion growth. That reality was eye opening and painful.

Believers were joining our ranks because they appreciated the Bible teaching, liked the music ministry, or had children in the youth programs. We were not experiencing Kingdom expansion but Kingdom redistribution. Or to say it in Las Vegas vocabulary, we were merely reshuffling the deck. Even among the conversions, most of them were children of members. It became obvious that we were not making a spiritual dent in Las Vegas. The hard-to-ignore data was sobering to our church leaders. We were investing prayer, money, hard work, and sacrifice, but the kingdom of God was not being expanded. Even though God had placed Central Church in the middle of one of America's greatest mission fields, almost no growth was coming from the spiritually pagan group. Something had to change.

EXPLORING THE OPTIONS

So what would we do? And when?

At that time, Central Church was experiencing the typical organizational S-curve. Here's how the S-curve works. An organization begins, as Central Church began in 1962, and struggles a bit at first. Then as they get through that struggle, they move on to growth and organizational health where things go well until they reach the top of the S-curve. Then they start down that *S*.

At that time, this question has to be processed: What does an organization have to do when they reach the top of the *S* if they wish to continue to fulfill their God-given purpose? The answer—they have to seriously relook at themselves and even reinvent themselves. They have to initiate a change process for a new era. That's where Central Church found itself. Refocusing was absolutely necessary. What were we going to do? What were the options?

For us, it really came down to about four possibilities.

Planting a new congregation was our first option. Then we could say, "We are not winning the lost to Christ, so we will plant a congregation that will be evangelistic."

A second option was to transplant a ministry off campus. Maybe go to a school or community building and start a special ministry away from the traditional setting.

A third option might be to implant a new ministry in the existing facility. That might mean starting a separate service targeting a different group. The new group might be generational, bicultural, or migrant people.

The fourth option would be to spiritually transform the entire church. This desirable option takes hard work, a clear understanding of what the church is supposed to be, and a determination to make it happen.

When we got to the top of the organizational S-curve, we chose to plant a church and seek spiritual transformation options. Several factors forced us to decide that God wanted to do both.

We chose church planting because southern Nevada is growing so rapidly. We realized there was no way in one congregation we could keep up with population growth. So we decided to aggressively plant churches. Since we wanted to birth healthy babies, we were not so concerned about planting a church every six months or every year as we were about planting healthy congregations. We are happily willing to allow God to determine the time schedule.

One of the big factors for us became the "eventually" question. That is, What are the long-term implications of our proposed course of action?

What are we going to do as the two congregations get older, and are we going to create two churches within a church? It's a great question, and it should be answered, but in Kingdom efforts, we must often move forward without all the answers. Some answers only come in process.

We decided we would like to see the whole church transformed today rather than wait until every detail was completely thought through. All the eventuality issues can only be determined by God for us.

I was the hit man for change. The first 10 years I was in Las Vegas I would describe myself as being the change hit man. I quickly learned that not everybody wanted to go with me. Some people get out of the boat before it even starts into the channel— probably because they are afraid—and others delay becoming change personalities until they see some positive results start to happen.

But many of the changes have started to pay off by making the church effective in reaching lost people. Let's consider what Central has become. There are so many differences. An effective seeker-targeted ministry style is in place. The organ is gone. No one sings in robes. Contemporary music, multimedia, drama, and video have become important components of worship. Six thousand gather every weekend and bring their seeking friends with them. A Wednesday night believers' service each week draws more than 1,800. Women have prominent roles in church life. One Elder Board has replaced the three-board concept. The small-group ministry, though nonexistent in those early years, has over 200 active adult groups.

*A major change initiative
without the full 110 percent
involvement and support of the
senior pastor is doomed.*

The most important difference for me is that present increases are 75 percent conversion growth, and even veteran believers who join our fellowship from other churches say, "We have dreamed all our lives of being a part of a church that reaches lost people; we want to be partners in what is happening." That, to my mind, is what has been the most significant improvement. We have moved from Kingdom redistribution to authentic Kingdom expansion.

TRANSITION PRINCIPLES THAT CAN WORK ANYWHERE

What are our transferable principles that could help other congregations get through the channel of change? What are some universal concepts for leading change that work no matter what the setting—rural, urban, suburban—and no matter what the size of a church? Here are some of the things I learned from the Central experience.

1. Senior pastor must be committed to change. You have to have a senior pastor who is willing and gifted to ride as the point person. A major change initiative without the full 110 percent involvement and support of the senior pastor is doomed. Anyone who has had any experience with change knows there are tricks people use to undermine change. They question methodology, theology, integrity, and sincerity. None of that is fun.

So for transitions to happen, the senior pastor must be committed to leading the change initiative. In our case, the initiative was to reach lost people. I would say often that *lost people matter* more than the criticism we are receiving.

I think back to a church I know well. The senior pastor had been there for 20 years; the church had grown to nearly 3,000 people. A number of their staff and lay leaders went to a leadership conference at Willow Creek Church. They came back all buzzed up, wanting to transition toward a Willow Creek model.

They proposed and started a Saturday night service and then quickly added a Wednesday night believer service. The senior pastor was so overwhelmed by their enthusiasm, he almost felt as if he had to get on board with it. Though he gave his nod to the changes, it was not 110 percent from his heart. When they started going through the channel of change, people came to the senior pastor with their fears, criticisms, and outright opposition. He started backing down. The long and short of it was that the senior pastor, who had done an incredible job, resigned. The church went back to the way things always had been. Now that church is light years away from being able to introduce transformational change because of such a bad experience. George Barna has a great chapter on turnaround pastors in his book *Turn Around Churches,* where he suggests several gifts or qualities are needed to become a turnaround pastor. Let me identify some of those qualities.

• *Youth.* Barna found one of the consistent characteristics was youth. Most effective turnaround pastors have led a church in a turnaround before the age of 45. The process is so demanding and takes so much energy that it helps to have a young pastor who has physical stamina.

• *Workaholism.* Turnaround churches typically have pastors who work 60 to 80 hours per week. While workaholism is not usually a desirable human trait, the frequent occurrence of this characteristic shows turnaround pastors are not afraid of hard work.

• *Spiritual commitment.* Barna discovered that turnaround pastors had an unusual devotion to developing an intimate relationship with God on a regular basis and to leading others to do the same.

• *Strong personality.* Most turnaround pastors are self-assured, self-confident persons who are not afraid to make tough decisions. They are the kind of persons others are willing to follow, even in tough times.

• *Potential visionary.* Barna found that even though many turnaround pastors had not necessarily demonstrated great vision in previous ministry, they possessed a potential visionary characteristic inside waiting to be expressed. Visionaries are able to see potential others may never recognize.

• *Length of service.* It takes time for the senior pastor to earn trust before leading a major change initiative, and no change works well without a high level of trust. Expect that the time factor will be different in every situation. If a pastor goes to a church that is on life support, he or she can probably initiate major changes pretty quickly. Or a pastor's unusual gifts may shorten the time-trust building factor; all of us have seen situations where a new senior pastor was such a gifted communicator or talented teacher that by their charming magnetism and commanding presence they were able to lead rapidly through strong change. Leaders like that, however, are extremely rare.

Typically, an established church that does not even know it is sick or weak may need up to three years to gain confidence in a new senior pastor's leadership. But a pastor should be careful about waiting too long. Once a pastor goes past the two-year point without initiating changes, a congregation gets used to a pastor's leadership style and will be slow to accept him or her as a change agent.

> *The success caused confidence in my leadership to go up and for people to trust me.*

When I arrived at Central Church, they had been without a pastor for at least a year. During that time, they launched a stewardship campaign to raise a million dollars to build a badly needed gymnasium and additional classrooms and to pay off some debt. The campaign was all lay led. They decided to do it without a consultant. About the time I came on the scene, they had the big finale of the $1 million goal campaign that had pledged $93,000 over a three-year period. They felt defeated. And now a 25-year-old pastor arrives, and they ask me, "What do we do?" Of course, I did not know, but I phoned some senior pastor friends and said, "Help!" They offered several suggestions. One was lower the goal. They told me if we did not use a consultant, our goal was too high.

So we set a new goal for $400,000 and called the campaign "Chart a New Course." We prayed hard as I cast a vision for a new era of ministry. We had an all-church banquet at a hotel. That night of the banquet, just about the time I arrived home, those who tabulated the pledges called to report we went over $400,000 in our commitments.

Well, a big "Praise God" went up from the church family, especially from the lay leaders.

What happened was this. Though I had been there only a short time, was only 25 years old and still pretty suspect, the crisis of the previous campaign made people more willing to follow me. The success caused confidence in my leadership to go up and for people to trust me. Every pastor needs a few experiences like that—small hills to help him or her gain the confidence of the people. Though I did not fully realize it then, this first win made me realize we could achieve what I dreamed of doing. It also built momentum for future projects.

To be an effective change-agent pastor, one must be able to pilot a congregation through the first few feet in the change channel to help them see the opportunities.

Another benefit among negative, doubting people is underscored by John P. Kotter, author of *Leading Change.* He advises that "quick performance improvements undermine the efforts of cynics and major league resisters. Wins do not necessarily quiet all of these people, but they take some of the ammunition out of opponents' hands and make it much more difficult to take cheap shots at those trying to implement needed changes. As a general rule, the more cynics and resisters, the more important are short-term wins."

Several years later, when we were about ready to cross that finish line on several buildings, I knew it was going to take several millions of dollars to finish. Until then, I never thought of myself as a fund-raiser. But in order to finish this type of project, I realized I was going to have to personally ask some people if they would be open to what God might be able to do through them. The very first time I asked for a gift on a person-to-person basis, I called a family in our church to ask if I could take them out to dinner. Instead, they invited me to their house. At their table I cast the vision and he asked, "How are you going to finance it?" I said it's funny you should ask that, and I laid out how we were going to be asking the congregation, but I continued, "We really need someone to give up-front gifts to set the pace." I told him that's why I was there—to ask if he would prayerfully consider giving a gift between $500,000 and $1 million. Without missing a beat in the conversation, he said that we could count on him for $1 million. After they picked me up off the floor, we had a great evening of fellowship. My confidence was real high in asking for gifts after that dinner because I realized that God could direct us to people who would help fund every worthwhile effort.

Another factor that helped me gain confidence is that I always worked hard at my preaching ministry. When I went to Central, a well-loved senior pastor advised me, "Gene, great preaching covers a multitude of sins." And he is right. Not many books about growing healthy churches say much about the importance of preaching. Perhaps it is just assumed. I believe preaching more than any other function of my ministry has helped me navigate many of our church's changes.

I believe that Charles Spurgeon's advice needs to be applied today: "Have something to say, and say it earnestly, and the congregation will be at your feet" (Anthony J. Ruspantini, ed. *Quotable Spurgeon*). Or to put the idea in more contemporary terms, people will still come to hear thoughtful and applicable truth from the preacher.

2. Casting a vision for the future. Once God begins to plant a vision in a leader's heart, it soon moves to a second leader, a third leader, a team of leaders, and then the whole congregation.

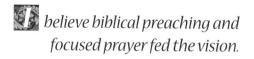 *believe biblical preaching and focused prayer fed the vision.*

Change = dissatisfaction × vision × the first step. Change happens when there is dissatisfaction with the way things are. Change starts when a leader asks, how can things be better?

Then the first few steps must be viewed as being achievable. So you can start moving toward your goal when you have dissatisfaction with the status quo, a stated vision, and a belief that the first few steps are achievable.

How did that play out at Central Church? In our case, it started with the conversion statistics. When we realized that our growth was only 25 percent by conversion, we were dissatisfied.

Even persons who feared change the most started asking, "What can we do as a church to reach more people?" I spent a large part of my first 60 sermons from the Book of Acts—the longest sermon series I have ever done. As a result, a biblical vision formed, inspiring us all to see how things could be better and closer to the New Testament pattern. Our church became vibrant and anointed with the power of the Holy Spirit.

Then a new interest in prayer started. I believe biblical preaching and focused prayer fed the vision. As the Holy Spirit helped me state the vision and helped lay leaders apply it, change began to emerge.

3. **A perceptive analysis of what is possible and when.** The old spiritual says, "You gotta move when the Spirit moves." In practical terms, that means there is a window of opportunity when something can be done that can never be done as effectively again. It is a just-right time to move that is neither too soon nor too late. Part of the danger of a few days at a conference or exposure to a powerful new book is that your vision expands. Then you go back to your congregation and you spill it out. Soon the people get sick of hearing about it because you are likely talking concepts and ideas rather than implementation and achievement.

> *Many wonderful Kingdom-expansion proposals have never been implemented because the leader used the wrong timing.*

Here's how it works. You discover something fresh that may even be life changing for you. But people of the congregation wonder, "Where did that come from, and why does it matter to us?"

Following TV host David Letterman's pattern, I came up with a list of top-five mistakes to avoid after you have been to a conference.

No. 5: Go home and tell your board you had a $90 million vision.

No. 4: Chastise anyone who disagrees with you as not giving a rip about lost people.

No. 3: Start trying to look like Rick Warren or Bill Hybels.

No. 2: Tuck into every conversation something about Asbury Seminary and the Beeson International Center for Biblical Preaching and Church Leadership.

No. 1: Rename one of your leaders Dale Galloway.

No—to make progress, you must be impacted by an idea and then develop a strategy to get it implemented. Be smart and savvy about what is appropriate when. What and when are always connected—thus timing is an important but often overlooked factor in decision making. Many wonderful Kingdom-expansion proposals have never been implemented because the leader used the wrong timing.

I think of the change process as being like two mountains— Old Paradigm or Traditional Mountain and New Paradigm or Cutting-Edge Mountain. People usually have to get sufficiently dissatisfied with the old mountain before they are willing to climb the new one. That is not to say or even imply that their present mountain has never been a good one. People have a vested interest in the old mountain, and many remember how hard it was to climb. It has served the church well, and some may have even dedicated their lives to it. For example, the church building is the place where the lost were found, believers grew, and God was exalted. Even if its serious space limitations were acknowledged, it would be hard for a person to see a sanctuary sold or demolished where he or she found Christ and was married and where the funerals for two generations of his or her family were held.

Problems like this get magnified, threatening, or even insulting when a change agent shows up to lead a transition in the church and says a new mountain must be climbed. The new person who knows little about the past paints a vision of everybody climbing this new mountain together. This change agent promises great views and changed lives. He or she speaks about a new day in the life of the church, and, without intending to do so, implies the old mountain was irrelevant.

Consider what this sounds like to the people in the pews. They hear a person saying, "You folks have been climbing the wrong mountain all these years. You have given your time, prayers, and money to the wrong mountain." And the congregation knows better.

Does the phrase "digging in your heels" ring a bell in your mind as you think about the two mountains? Often people resist going to the new mountain just because the familiar has been good to them, and they resent a new pastor trying to destroy what they love.

To make the challenge to climb the new mountain less stressful, change-agent pastors need to work hard to create a paradigm shift. Not only do they have to motivate people to believe there is an exciting new mountain to climb, but they also have to convince them to come down from the old mountain. One without the other causes unnecessary resistance and opposition.

This mountain concept helps me analyze where we are as a church when considering initiating change. Who is on which mountain? Where is my staff right now? Where are the board members? Where are the key leaders? Where are the opinion leaders in the church? And where is the membership of the church? This thought process is a good analysis tool for me.

Let me give you some examples of doing a perceptive analysis of what's appropriate and when.

I am often asked, "Gene, when you went to Central, did you inform your leaders that it was your desire to transform the church with a seeker-targeted ministry?" The answer—No, I didn't tell them. It was 1985, and in those days no one knew what a seeker-targeted ministry was. I didn't even know. Though I was not sure the church had the capacity to transition, I went with the idea of seeing what God wanted us to do together. Over the years, it became clear to me that it would be possible to transition to a new paradigm together. Another factor has to be considered. A perceptive analysis of what's appropriate when reminds me that no one would allow a 10-year-old to drive an Indy car. That 10-year-old may grow into a wonderful race car driver, but not yet. That growing child is not ready for Indy yet and may never be. Some good Christian people may never be ready to lead the charge for change in a church. That does not mean they are bad people, but that they cannot lead change any more than a child can drive a race car. However, these same people may enjoy the new mountain after others have led the congregation to get there.

Another example of analysis and timing took place when we moved our weekend services to the gymnasium. Our sanctuary, with its stained-glass windows and crosses on every light fixture, was not a conducive environment for reaching seekers. I thought the gym, with its theatrical lighting, curtains, and stage, would provide a more neutral environment to preach the gospel. But since the gym seated 300 more people, I looked ahead and could see it was only a matter of time until our growth would force us to move the service there. So I waited for the inevitable. In six months, we were forced to change and avoided a great blow up. By then it was obvious what needed to be done. Leaders have to be perceptive about what's appropriate when.

To understand the importance of timing, it may be useful to consider Central Church's time line. The period 1985-87 was the time frame when new values were taking root and a new vision was being born—a time when our congregation was becoming dissatisfied with mere maintenance ministry. The new vision became more clear in '88 and '89 as we started to see how some first few steps of change could be started. The year 1990 was the time we started implementing several transformational changes. A leadership storm hit in '91 and '92—we were in the middle of the channel of change and had major confusion. Some lost courage because they could not see where the ship was headed. From '93 to the present I would describe as the joy of persevering. Though change is not over, there is the joy of seeing spiritual fruit from the transitions, even the painful ones.

4. Balance persistence and patience. This is hard for pastors who thrive on change, controversy, or confrontation. Since you are a change agent, it is difficult to be patient but persistent.

Someone said that patience is passion tamed. That perspective helps me. Never lose sight of the ultimate goal, but tame impulsive attitudes and destructive actions when congregants change too slowly. It's a hard lesson to learn, but few if any of your leaders or members will change as quickly as you wish they would.

I am convinced, though, that with a balance of patience and persistence, you can get 80 to 90 percent of the people on board. I tell my congregation, "We're going to take three steps forward and go right out to the edge of this wedge of change—a place where we have never been." When you get out there, some will think it is uncomfortable. Then the wise transitional leader will say, "I know how you feel. We don't have to stay out here. Let's take a step or two back." Everybody will sigh, "Whew! This feels a lot better." Then with a little patience and persistence, you can take another wedge of change a little while later. In the process, you are making progress.

I would describe the process of transitioning the typical church as a series of steps like that. It is often three steps forward, two steps backward—over and over again. Then one day you wake up and you are a different church than you used to be. It happens subtly over time.

An example—back in the early '90s we used a song called "Show Me the Way," which expressed the cry of the seeker. The style and tempo were more rock and roll and radical than anything we had ever used. Several people said after that service that it made them feel uncomfortable. So we stepped back a few steps. But about a year later, we used that exact song, and there was no feeling of anyone being uncomfortable with it. Change took place over time, and we avoided a divisive war over nothing.

THE BOTTOM LINE OF TRANSITIONING CHURCHES

I want to express a strong conviction. I know there is a temptation for some who serve in traditional settings to jump ship and go start a new church. If that's God's call for you, I hope you'll obey it. We need lots of new churches, but thousands of existing churches need resurrection, renewal, and revolution. New churches and renewed churches have the same goals—win the lost and make disciples. Both are desperately needed.

Here's my take on the transition question of established but nonproductive churches. North America has many churches that have land, buildings, people, and finances. Isn't it good stewardship to allow God to use us to awaken this sleeping giant?

I never want to forget that after we had initiated all these changes in our church, a cocktail waitress from the Mirage Hotel began attending our services. She found a church that started with her where she was and pointed her toward where she needed to be. The people loved her and communicated with her in a way she could understand. She kept coming, and before long she gave her life to Christ. I will never forget the day she was baptized. She had invited a number of her friends to be with her for this spiritual milestone. Afterward, they gathered for a group picture in front of our baptistery.

What a picture it was—30 cocktail waitresses from the Mirage Hotel and Casino gathered in front of our baptistery for a group picture. I believe that Jesus loved the scene even more than I did.

I remember thanking God for a church that has had the courage to change, remembering that lost people matter to Him, and that has been willing to go through the change channel with Him.

That's our story.

·9·

TRANSITIONING TO A NEW LOCATION

Jim Garlow

The soul without imagination is what
an observatory would be without a telescope.
—**Harry Williams**

God and change are the only two abiding facts in every life and church" is the incredibly accurate observation of a wise old church leader. He is right. He fully understood that great Kingdom accomplishments happen when change and God are creatively connected. From long experience, he also understood that every significant accomplishment for Christ requires change on someone's part. By refusing to deal with these realities, many pastors and their congregations have undermined the effectiveness of their ministries.

I WAS A BEGINNER AT TRANSITIONS

Before moving to Skyline Church, I thought I knew how transitions worked. I even thought of myself as a change agent. After all, I was a pastor who founded a church that appealed to contemporary boomers. I took great satisfaction in the ways our church was different from other churches—even cutting edge, you understand. But Skyline made me realize I was actually inexperienced at understanding and using transitions.

As founding pastor of Metroplex Chapel in the Dallas-Fort Worth area, I was intensely focused on growing a great church. I had noble dreams for the church's future. I thought I would be there the rest of my life. Since I started the church, few changes were needed.

Then the call came to San Diego. The process of changing locations and moving from a church I had planted to a church with a long and effective history forced me to deal in an experiential way with how transitions work and what changes do to individuals and churches.

In the process, I felt an inner pressure, perhaps even a directive from God, to develop an understanding of how a pastor can use the transition experiences for sharpening his or her personal ministry, for leading a church to a productive future, while not harming the church he or she is leaving.

In this era when change has become more and more constant, many churches maintain an antichange mind-set. Sometimes their fear of change is rooted in inaccurate memories of "good ole days." Resistence may even come from the inaccurate notion that a change of method dilutes the message. However, an unsettling fact has to be recognized: the church that refuses to deal positively with transitions is either dead or dying. And that applies to church leaders as well.

Build on your experience. As I reflect about those years in the Dallas-Fort Worth area, the church—like churches everywhere—was in a constant state of transition. New people, recurring problems, cultural changes, potential crises, major opportunities, frustrating obstacles—nothing was the same or predictable for long.

So when God directed me to this new assignment at Skyline Church in San Diego, I began a demanding and sometimes frustrating transitional personal journey. But some of the basic elements were already part of my experience. In these experiences, I began to understand that the nature of change is a way of life. A pastor friend I greatly admire likes to say, "The church is always in a state of transition."

Transitions impact many people. Every pastoral change creates trauma for many people. Depending on the size of the congregation, scores and maybe hundreds of individuals are forced to rethink many things. Often they revisit or reduce their involvement in stewardship and service.

Personally, a pastor feels grief and guilt at leaving and anticipation and fear at arriving. For the minister, transition creates an in-between experience that feels like the trapeze artist forced to let go of one bar while reaching for another.

The pastor's family must adjust to find new friends, move to a different house often selected by others, attend a new school, go to new doctors, and learn to love a new congregation.

he not-so-obvious challenge of the transition process is to find ways to make it a growth experience for you and your people.

Lay leaders in both churches have to learn to work with a new minister who may be as different as daylight and dark from their previous pastor. Church staffs face uncertain futures. New converts feel they are losing a trusted friend. Aging saints wonder how well the new pastor does funerals. Starry-eyed young people who always thought the pastor would be there for their weddings and the dedication of their babies feel abandoned. Even the casual church visitor faces disappointment by changes in preaching and worship caused by the pastor's leaving. Emotions such as grief, separation, anxiety, sadness, anticipation, and even terror flow across an entire congregation.

Meanwhile, a similar range of emotions takes place in the church that awaits the new pastor. They feel loss and grief for their previous pastor. And in the midst of the separation, they feel forced to smile through their tears to welcome their new pastor.

Using transitions for personal growth. The not-so-obvious challenge of the transition process is to find ways to make it a growth experience for you and your people. Use it as a time to learn new lessons about God, about people, and about the church you serve. Use it as an opportunity to develop new skills of self-understanding and to discover God's plans for your new church. Use it to develop strong pastor-people connections in the people of God. Use it to draw close to your own family.

Since God is constant in every change, I found strength for my transition from Ps. 46 that says, "God is our refuge and strength, an ever-present help in trouble. Therefore we will not fear, though the earth give way and the mountains fall into the heart of the sea, though its waters roar and foam and the mountains quake with their surging. . . . The Lord Almighty is with us; the God of Jacob is our fortress" (vv. 1-3, 7).

God's presence as our refuge in the details is a fact of life according to Scripture. Understanding that the Lord Almighty is with me and the God of Jacob is my fortress equips me with inner resources to deal with transitions when I am uncertain or even afraid of the details. As God resources us in the transitions, we can take heart that all will be well.

MAKE CHANGE A CHOICE

Since change is inevitable, make it a choice. Respond to it positively and creatively. Welcome it with anticipation instead of reacting to it as an intrusive enemy. Concepts such as *potentiality, anticipation, opportunities,* and *new beginnings* are needed and useful.

P astoral transition is like a relay. Successful relays are won by those who know how to pass on the baton with precision and accuracy.

Warren Bennis in *Why Leaders Can't Lead* offers this advice about how to build acceptance for change in yourself and others: "Change-oriented administrators are particularly prone to act as though the organization came into being the day they arrived. This is a delusion, a fantasy of omnipotence. There are no clean slates in established organizations. . . . some of the old hands have, besides knowledge and experience, real creativity."

Pastoral change is periodic change. In my transition from Metroplex Chapel to Skyline Church, I prepared a booklet for the church I was leaving and the one to which I was going. I choose to call transition a relay and expanded the idea like this:

Pastoral transition is like a relay. A relay consists of four runners and a baton. Speed is important but not the most important thing. The transition is critical. Four fast runners who cannot properly hand on the baton will lose. Four good runners who understand transition will win. Successful relays are won by those who know how to pass on the baton with precision and accuracy.

My part of the race at Metroplex Chapel is now ending. The race here is now yours. At this point it matters less how fast we run as how carefully we hand the baton. I pass it on to you now, challenging you to first carefully receive the baton, and only then—when you have it firmly in your grip—to run the race as fast as you can.

John Maxwell, former pastor at Skyline, wrote this: "Trust is the glue that holds a leader and the organization together. When I handed the baton off to Jim, we made a commitment to trust each other. This has given a great sense of security to the congregation. Jim Garlow is my pastor and my very good friend."

Dan Huckins, who followed me at Metroplex, wrote these words:

After transitioning into Metroplex Chapel, I learned three things very quickly. First, I learned Jim Garlow had left a wonderful legacy. I was indeed standing on his shoulders. Second, he had thoroughly prepared the people, especially the leadership, to receive me and my leadership and style with open arms. Following a pastor and leader of his stature, this was critical. Third, after being at Metroplex Chapel for a while, I realized Jim Garlow could be my pastor anytime. I thank him for transitioning in such a way that I could be effective in the church he founded. That is a great gift.

Then in my efforts to make the transition smooth and effective, I wrote the following:

Ten Commandments for a Pastor When Leaving a Church

1. Talk with key lay leaders privately before the public announcement. They deserve some process time, even if only 24 hours. Yes, it might "leak," but it's worth the risk.

2. When you make the announcement, say it in the first

sentence, then explain later. Do not build up to it slowly, causing unnecessary apprehension.

3. Keep explanations simple and straightforward. Complex reasons for leaving only confuse people. Assure them you are following the will of God as best you understand it.

4. Don't stay around long. Leave within six weeks or earlier. You are worth nothing after two or three weeks. In fact, your presence may even hurt.

5. Don't promise you will be there for weddings or funerals. Contrary to what you and they think, they will do fine without you.

6. Don't "wind down." Keep the preaching positive. Tell them God will see them through this, because He will.

7. Don't publicly mention the church you are going to more than a couple of times. They will tire of it quickly after the third time. They are focused on their future, not yours.

8. Don't "stack the deck" for who is to follow you. Give the church board a long list of suggestions for your successor and persons to call for leads. They need this, as you know more pastors than they do. Then get out of the way.

9. Don't attack your critics. You left behind a lot of good fruit. Remember, vengeance is the Lord's.

10. Don't criticize their choice of a new pastor. Affirm their decision no matter who they pick as your successor. This will help him or her succeed. Then rejoice when they do!

Ten Commandments for a Pastor Going to a New Church

1. Enjoy the honeymoon. A honeymoon isn't meant to last forever. And it won't.

2. Don't act like the Messiah. You are just "the next pastor." It's OK not to have lots of answers.

3. Never condemn the previous pastor's methods. His or hers were right, for him or her. Methods are never sacred, only the message.

4. Never yield to the temptation of making yourself look good at your predecessor's expense. Avoid the phrase, "When I came . . . (then describe how bad it was)." The former pastor's friends will resent this practice, and his or her enemies will distrust you.

5. Acknowledge your predecessor's hard work. To undermine any previous pastor's work makes people question your authenticity.

6. Acknowledge you are "standing on his [or her] shoulders," because you are. The building, people, and finances were either brought or at least maintained by him or her.

7. Do not try to be your predecessor. Be yourself. God gifts every leader in unique ways to serve His Church. Use your abilities for the glory of God.

8. Make some changes quickly, others slowly—and have the sense to know the difference. Take your time in most changes. Establish your priorities and make them clear. Put your philosophy of ministry in print so the people will know where you are taking the church.

9. Realize that you and your family will experience culture shock. You will wake up some mornings, possibly for as long as three years, wondering, "What have I done?" But it will be OK. You obeyed God, and He will see you through.

10. Understand that your "learning curve" or "finding your full stride" may take up to three years. So relax. You are in it for the long haul. Or at least you ought to be, because He is.

DEVELOP MENTAL/CULTURAL TRANSITION

The church must continually reinvent itself in a manner that is understood by the current culture. That requires transition. Thoughtful leaders both inside and outside the church believe significant changes take place about every four years in contemporary society. Thus, effective leaders try to understand what is happening in the culture so they can find effective ways to share the gospel of Christ in words and actions contemporary people understand. The issue is not to make the church like the culture, but to be able to speak the culture's language as an attempt to win more people for Christ.

DISCOVERY AND EVALUATION

Every pastor must develop an evaluation/assessment strategy when he or she goes to a new assignment. The idea is that the most critical areas get priority.

When I arrived at Skyline, the first thing I did was to become acquainted with every ministry of the church. Every church has ministry strengths and weaknesses.

- **Current strengths.** Skyline Church was very healthy because John Maxwell and his leadership team were phenomenally competent and creative.

Skyline's greatest strengths were strong lay leaders, a prayer partner ministry, one-on-one discipleship, and a general esprit de corps that ran throughout the church, especially in the adult Sunday School classes.

> *or me the defining question was, What areas in your church most need attention that will produce the strongest Kingdom impact?*

- **Areas that can wait.** In the assessment process, find out which ministry areas do *not* need your immediate focused attention. Every church has areas of ministry that need attention but can wait until a later time. I call those level-two and level-three areas. One of those was the college ministry.

At Skyline, the college ministry had taken a terrific hit, declining from 300 to 20 about a year before I came. I would love to have worked on that area of ministry, but many of the college students had graduated and were irretrievable. The drop happened because an extremely popular college pastor left a couple years earlier. I knew I had to put that area of ministry on the back burner temporarily because of the urgency of several other areas.

- **Areas that need immediate attention.** Focus on these. Giving immediate attention to these areas produces the strongest impact.

When I arrived at Skyline, I focused on six areas for the first 18 months. For me the defining question was, What areas in your church most need attention that will produce the strongest Kingdom impact?

Children. Due to Skyline's severe relocation challenges the children's facilities were inadequate. Approximately 15 percent of our Sunday morning attendance was children. I desired for at least

25 percent of the Sunday morning attendance to be children under the sixth grade. So we focused strongly on children's ministry. Consequently our Sunday morning attendance is now 24 percent children under the sixth grade—only 1 percent from our goal.

I wanted to design a children's ministry with a big "wow factor." What is a "wow factor"? My youngest children will hardly let us drive by the golden arches of McDonald's because of the wow factor. The wow factor is what makes a kid turn to his or her mother and say, "Mom, look. Wow." That is precisely the response I wanted children to have at church.

Within 10 days after I arrived at Skyline, I challenged the congregation to raise $100,000 to transform a rather nondescript courtyard and give it a Disney World look. The next step was to redesign the children's auditorium into a "Grand Central Station" with trains running along the sides. Focusing completely on children, we saw the number of younger families increase almost immediately.

When we were finally able to relocate to our new property in 2000, we designed a children's building that looks as if it was designed by Walt Disney!

Relocation. The second area that needed attention was relocation of our church. The original Skyline campus was located in a rapidly changing neighborhood.

Skyline's relocation had been a long struggle with many difficulties and disappointments. The struggle continued from 1981 to 2000. The church raised $2 million and bought land. Then they raised an additional $5 million, but it was consumed without turning a shovelful of dirt, due to environmental complications and bureaucratic topographical problems.

I knew that the church needed some tangible wins on relocation. They had experienced a decade and a half of disappointments. Some even believed that the church never would be able to build on its new property.

Here is an overview of the environmental and bureaucratic issues our church faced:

1. The Black Tailed Gnat Catcher, a so-called "endangered" bird. Two of them nested on the church's property. That fact will cost the church millions of dollars before we are finished. We are

not even allowed to do construction between February and August because that is the breeding season for these birds.

2. Unusable land. The church owns 130 acres on both sides of the freeway. We wanted to sell the land on the lower side of the freeway. But because the birds are on the land, it was declared "open space," which means we cannot sell it or develop it.

3. A bush. The property also has coastal sage on it, a small brown bush. We cannot build a building where coastal sage is growing.

4. The rock. A black rock was discovered on the property, which was believed to have been darkened by a bonfire built by Native Americans 2,000 years ago. As a result, 17 parking places in our lot were taken, and for perpetuity that property can never be used because some more blackened rocks might be found there!

5. The shard. A pottery shard was discovered, the size of my thumbnail. We are required to do a $120,000 archeological excavation, the 29th archeological dig on our property.

6. The mitigation canal. We own 130 acres, but we are only allowed to build on 25. The two birds get the rest of the property. And then we had to purchase 25 acres out in the mountains for $150,000 and turn that over to an environmental trust (in hopes that the two birds will be able to find it!).

7. The additional property. We had an opportunity to purchase 8 additional acres next to our property. Our plan was to pave it so we could park an additional 800 cars. That would keep us from having to build a multilevel parking garage, saving us millions of dollars. We bought the 8 acres for $250,000. We discovered, however, that we will never be able to legally walk on the property because of more environmental difficulties.

8. Earthquake laws. Before we were able to begin our first building, earthquake laws changed, thus requiring $856,000 more in steel and concrete.

9. Blue granite. When we tried to blast the mountain building out, we ran into a vein of blue granite, which is six times stronger than concrete. This increased our earthmoving contract from $1 million to over $2 million.

10. The freeway. We were required to add two lanes to the

freeway that runs seven-tenths of a mile through our property. This project cost $3 million.

11. More environmental complications. Our campus design calls for six structures. Our first building was a $6 million structure. But due to environmental complications we paid $26 million to build it.

By 1997, the congregation had been through four financial campaigns and never turned one shovel of dirt on the property.

It was obvious that Skyline Church needed their new leader to give them some sense of security that this was a doable project.

In all candor, this relocation challenge was a major reason I was hesitant to come to Skyline as pastor. But God gave me a verse from Ps. 20:7 that says, "Some boast in chariots, some in horses; But [you] will boast in the name of the LORD" (NASB).

Let me ask you a question?
What ministries in your church
need you to focus like a laser beam
to give your church a sense of
security and confidence?

From the start I realized this project was over my head. Following John Maxwell as pastor was over my head. Financing relocation was over my head. This is the first time in my life I have been in a situation where I had to say, "I cannot do this job." That is what I told them when they called on May 1, 1995. But God gave me the promise that if we boast in the name of Jesus, He would take us through. Little by little, we gained "mountain momentum."

My question to you: Though you may not be involved in relocation, what areas in your church really need your hands-on support as senior pastor? What needs your focused attention? What ministries in your church need you to focus like a laser beam to give your church a sense of security and confidence?

Times and locations. The third ministry that needed my immediate attention was the times and locations of services. When I became pastor at Skyline, there were four services. One service, held on the main campus, met at 10:40 on Sunday morning. That should have been a good time, but we could not get it to grow even though our other three services were doing well. After much effort, we abandoned that service and created one that was more vital and attractive.

> *According to church growth specialist Chip Arn, fear is the primary blockage against starting a new service.*

Here's what we did: (1) We moved its location into a school near our future site. (2) We arranged time schedules of all services so the senior pastor can meet and greet worshipers following each service (even though we were on two campuses). (3) We limited services to one hour and five minutes per service. (4) We did not start the first service before 8 A.M. nor end the last service past 12:15 P.M. (5) We added a Saturday night service.

For many pastors, it is a surprise to learn that the shape, energy, and anointing of the worship service, its location, and the time of meeting determine how many people will show up.

According to church growth specialist Chip Arn, fear is the primary blockage against starting a new service. I struggled with my fears that a new Saturday night service would not work. But we began it, and it has given us another verve for growth.

The second blockage for starting a new service is a pastor's unwillingness to allocate time for it. Of course, any new service takes time to lead. But there is also the time needed for preparation, setup, and greeting the people.

Here is my question for you: Are your worship times postured, located, and scheduled for maximum Kingdom impact?

Thought tailored specifically for your situation, our guidelines might provide a sample for other churches. They are as follows:

1. Develop new worship services toward where we are "going," not where we're "leaving."

2. Keep all Sunday worship services between 8 A.M. and noon.

3. Allow the senior pastor to greet after all services if possible.

4. Allow one hour and five minutes per service.

5. Maintain identical services in excellence—even if type of service varies.

P ray until you weep over your city.

Extroversion. The fourth area that needed attention was "extroversion." All churches drift toward introversion. They experienced exponential growth during the '80s. But the church plateaued during the '90s.

How do you get a church to grow that has gone through several years of plateau and decline?

For me, the key was to develop a city vision based on Luke 19:41, where Jesus looked at the city and wept.

Let me ask you, When is the last time you as pastor wept over your city? What do you see when you see this city? To help our church get a burden for our city, I use a four-letter slogan—CITI-Vision (care, invite, touch, and include).

C equals care. Care equals earnest prayer for your city. Pray until you weep over your city. Jesus did, why not you?

I equals invite. There is something profoundly powerful about a personal invitation. Almost all the new persons who pray and receive Christ in our services were invited by somebody. And their lives are forever changed.

T equals touch. Touch them at the point of their need. Find the need and meet it.

I equals include. Include people into your life flow and into the life flow of the congregation. Many Christians are not aware that our world is full of unchurched or unsaved persons whom we can win to Christ by including them in the friendship of the family of God.

Presence and care. My fifth immediate goal was to establish presence and express care. My question: Knowing your members experience constant flux and change, what can you do to bring about stability and security at church? Our people are hit with so much change. What can you do to offset that?

The purpose was to increase a feeling of stability and security in a church that had changed its senior pastor and 12 pastoral staff members in two years. That's an extremely high trauma for a church. John Vaughan of the International Mega Church Research Center says that high visibility staff changes can affect a church by as much as 10 percent of its attendance.

John Maxwell's leaving was hard on Skyline Church because they loved him very much. Three highly visible staff members who were very connected with the congregation also left at the same time. That was a painful time for the church. So I began to work aggressively on trying to develop a sense of stability and permanence.

I worked to establish "presence" with the congregation. I let them know they matter not only to God but to me as well. I let them know how honored I was to serve them. I loved being with them and wanted to be able to greet them by name.

Stability also grows when people know where you are leading them. It took some time for me to clearly formulate my "agenda," but when it finally emerged, I was able to declare it with passion and confidence. The goal of Skyline was to help people know Christ by (1) experiencing His love, (2) enjoying His family, (3) knowing His ways, (4) being His person, and (5) doing His work. Everything we do is built around these 5 areas.

"Experiencing His love" is the area of our training that produces passion for Christ. "Enjoying His family" is the relationship building track. "Knowing His ways" is growth strategy that is designed to stimulate one's intellect in Bible, theology, and church history. "Being His person" is a growth strategy to produce integrity, righteousness, and heart holiness. And "doing His work" is a lay ministry development track.

In this section, I have shown ways I try to create a sense of presence and care at Skyline. But you may need to do something different to accomplish the same purposes. Here are three key questions:

• What are the ways I let the people of my congregation know that they are special to me?

• How often do I express the vision of our church in understandable ways?

• In what ways do I usually answer the often unstated question—Where are we going?

W̲h̲at do you need to develop in order to maximize your effectiveness?

Optimum effectiveness. The sixth immediate goal was to discover and develop my personal optimum effectiveness for my ministry at Skyline. My personal goal is to function at maximum effectiveness for Kingdom achievement. To accomplish that goal, I had to determine the things I needed to jettison and to discover ways I was going to stretch as a person.

I had to let go of a hobby that I love—politics. When I lived in Dallas-Fort Worth, Texas, I knew almost everybody who ran for public office. I invited them all to my church. I attempted to meet them. I have loved politics since I was a nine-year-old.

I knew that I had to let go of other things in order to develop. I was following John Maxwell, who has the capacity to identify key leaders of the church, draw them in, and develop them. I realized I needed to develop in this area. I was able to identify potential leaders, but I found it more difficult to develop a strategy to develop them. I am being forced to stretch in a way that is good, but difficult, for me.

My question to you is, What do you need to develop in order to maximize your effectiveness? What do you need to give up? What things do you need to "jettison"? How do you need to stretch? What skills do you need to develop?

Every new ministry assignment requires you to grow, to stretch, to give up, to add to, to become. What a joy to realize that God is continually at work modeling, shaping, and challenging us to greater usefulness.

Reading my story is far less important than your knowing

your story—than your hearing God's guidance about transition-ing that needs to happen in your local church so you and your congregation can have maximum Kingdom impact on your com-munity.

Here's my prayer—and one I trust will be meaningful for you: Father, our churches are not ours. They are Yours. Even if we stay a long time in our pastorates, it is still a short window of time on Your calendar of eternity. One of these days our names will be taken off the front sign. Somebody else's name will go up, and another transition will take place. The congregation will stop for five minutes, use a Kleenex or two, and move on. There is a heart cry within us to exalt Jesus over our cities, over our vil-lages, and over our rural areas. We ask that Your Holy Spirit will inspire our concepts and deepen our understandings so we may serve Your Church better. Amen.